Sex Discrimination and Law Firm
Culture on the Internet

Sex Discrimination and Law Firm Culture on the Internet

Lawyers at the Information Age Watercooler

Amanda K. Baumle

palgrave
macmillan

SEX DISCRIMINATION AND LAW FIRM CULTURE ON THE INTERNET
Copyright © Amanda K. Baumle, 2009.

First published in 2009 by
PALGRAVE MACMILLAN®
in the United States—a division of St. Martin's Press LLC,
175 Fifth Avenue, New York, NY 10010.

Where this book is distributed in the UK, Europe and the rest of the
world, this is by Palgrave Macmillan, a division of Macmillan Publishers
Limited, registered in England, company number 785998, of Houndmills,
Basingstoke, Hampshire RG21 6XS.

Palgrave Macmillan is the global academic imprint of the above companies
and has companies and representatives throughout the world.

Palgrave® and Macmillan® are registered trademarks in the United States,
the United Kingdom, Europe and other countries.

ISBN: 978–0–230–61325–6

Library of Congress Cataloging-in-Publication Data

Baumle, Amanda K.
    Sex discrimination and law firm culture on the internet : lawyers at
the information age watercooler / by Amanda K. Baumle.
        p. cm.
    Includes bibliographical references and index.
    ISBN 978-0-230-61325-6
        1. Women lawyers—United States. 2. Sex discrimination against
women—United States. 3. Law firms—Social aspects—United States.
4. Sex role in the work environment—United States. 5. Internet—Social
aspects. I. Title.

KF299.W6B38 2009
340.082'0973—dc22   2008049763

A catalogue record of the book is available from the British Library.

Design by Newgen Imaging Systems (P) Ltd., Chennai, India.

First edition: June 2009

10 9 8 7 6 5 4 3 2 1

Transferred to Digital Printing in 2022

Contents

List of Figures and Tables

Figures

Tables

Acknowledgments

During my graduate study of qualitative methods, I took one of the basic premises of ethnographic research to heart and made the decision to study "what I know," that is, the legal practice. From the work conducted within my graduate program, I began to build the foundation for the research that was to become this manuscript.

Dr. Sarah Gatson's guidance throughout this work was invaluable, due in large part to her extensive knowledge and experience in conducting research in the areas of law and society, Internet ethnography, and gender inequality. I would also like to thank Dr. Gatson for demonstrating that it is possible to transform intellectual queries made during the course of everyday activities into exciting, scholarly work.

In addition, I would like to thank Dr. Dudley L. Poston, Jr., Dr. Mark Fossett, Dr. Barbara Sharf, Dr. Nancy Plankey Videla, and Dr. Joan Manley. These individuals served on my dissertation committee, out of which this research emerged. They provided valuable insight into issues related to gender and work, definitions of discrimination, Internet ethnography, and qualitative research methods. I appreciate their candor and thoughtful suggestions, which served to strengthen this work.

I would also like to extend my thanks to the editors at Palgrave Macmillan, Julia Cohen and Luba Ostashevsky, and the individuals selected as reviewers of this book. The editors' and reviewers' comments and suggestions resulted in improved clarity and academic quality. I would like to attribute credit to *shearmanditched*, a member of the Greedy Associates community, for coining the phrase used in the subtitle of this book: "Lawyers at the Information Age Watercooler" (*shearmanditched*, 9783, 12/14/01).

The artwork used for the cover of this book, "Mrs. Clinton at Work in Washington", was designed by Brian Piana and depicts an artistic interpretation of Senator Hillary Clinton's Web site; it was selected due to its focus on an Internet Web site and a woman attorney—two subjects of this work.

I would also like to acknowledge and give thanks for the support and advice provided by my friends, fellow graduate students, faculty, and staff in the Department of Sociology at Texas A&M University.

Finally, I would like to give special thanks to my husband, Larry, for his love and support during the course of this work.

I

Introduction

During my second year practicing law, I had the opportunity to depose my first witness. Dressed in a conservative black suit and carrying files and a briefcase, I arrived at the office of opposing counsel. The receptionist directed me to the appropriate conference room, and I soon struck up a conversation with the court reporter about the upcoming deposition. One of the opposing attorneys working on the case came by the office to determine whether the deposition was ready to proceed. He turned toward me and, as I stretched out my hand to introduce myself, he asked: "Are you the court reporter's sister? Did you come to watch her work?"

I was flustered and, at first, attributed his assumption to the fact that I was young and perhaps did not look of age to be an attorney. When I reconsidered the incident later that day, however, I realized that his conclusion had at least as much to do with my sex as with my age. Had the opposing counsel found a young man in the deposition room, dressed in a suit and surrounded by paperwork, it is improbable that he would have assumed that the court reporter's brother had accompanied her to learn about her work. This attorney, like many others, appeared to view women in the legal profession as secretaries, paralegals, or court reporters by default, and attorneys and judges only upon further offer of proof. The challenges facing women lawyers are noticeably engrained at many levels, to such an extent that a woman must, at times, establish her identity as an attorney, much less as a competent one. During my time practicing law, and since I left the law to pursue a career in academia, I learned of many incidents similar to this one—circumstances in which women lawyers encountered unique obstacles to their success compared to their male colleagues. Some of these experiences, such as my encounter with opposing counsel, simply reveal the male-dominated nature of the legal practice. These incidents are not actionable in a court of law, but can nonetheless influence interactions between opposing counsels, colleagues, and judges; at times, these influences can create additional barriers to success for women attorneys when handling a legal case. Other experiences, however, do constitute situations that are potential violations of state or federal antidiscrimination laws, including sex discrimination and sexual harassment.

Prior research has repeatedly documented the existence of gender inequality, discrimination, and harassment in the legal profession, an occupation that remains male-dominated both in terms of numbers and organizational culture (Pierce 1995; Rosenberg, Perlstadt, and Phillips 1993; Epstein 1970). Gender stereotyping, sex discrimination, and sexual harassment are all actionable under Title VII of the United States Civil Rights Act of 1965, as well as under many state laws. Despite the availability of legal remedies, however, women attorneys rarely sue their employers and often do not challenge discriminatory behavior. This book explores this seemingly contradictory situation, where lawyers fail to employ the legal system on their own behalf. In particular, I examine the manner in which attorneys navigate the process of determining whether to use (or to avoid) the law when opposing gender inequality in their employment. Ultimately, this research explores whether the law can be activated to challenge, and perhaps change, gender relations in the legal practice.

Rather than drawing data from interviews or surveys, data for this research come from the interactions of members of an Internet community. Attorneys use the Greedy Associates Web site community to engage in discussions concerning aspects of law firm life, including issues of gender inequality. Through ethnographic field research and content analysis of the online discourse, this book examines the manner in which attorneys consider the possible methods by which the law can serve as a tool to challenge gender discrimination. Further, I explore the manner in which the Internet community itself provides a unique forum for challenging gender inequality through appeals to legal rights.

My findings suggest that attorneys participating in the community are hesitant to employ formal litigation and face discouragement from their peers when litigation is proposed. The deterrents to formal litigation described by community members appear to be somewhat unique to the legal profession, generating a sense within the community that the law lacks utility in redressing such harms. The use of legal discourse in these situations, however, seems to show more promise, especially in the context of the Greedy Associates community. Generalized notions of rights are flexible and can be transformed by the oppressed into symbols for mobilization and for change (Lee 2001; Bourdieu and Thompson 1991). Bourdieu and Thompson (1991) observe that language, in addition to being a means of communication, is a source of symbolic power that is deployed by individuals in a manner dependent on the particular situated context; thus, individuals can adapt language to advance their own interests in political or social pursuits. As a result, Lee (2001:869) contends that "linguistic agency [i.e., the ability to define words in new ways]...provides an alternative to the relentless search for legal remedy."

When movements by the oppressed advancing new understandings of hegemony gain significant momentum, those in power are forced to a compromise and, thus, to a rearticulation of hegemony (Omi and Winant 1994). If this happens, both the specific definitions of racial or gender identities are reformed, as well as the relationships between those identities. Attorneys might, then, be able to call upon generalized notions of legal rights to mobilize individuals to pressure for change within law firm practices, forcing a rearticulation of gender identities and relationships within the legal practice.

This research focuses on examining whether the use of legal discourse by members of the Greedy Associates community could serve as a medium for change. Specifically, I explore the manner in which the Web site community allows attorneys to assert claims to "legal rights," as well as possible methods of instigating change through appeals to legal rights. Prior research examining the power of legal discourse has, at times, explored the role of attorneys in helping the oppressed to formulate their claims (e.g., McCann 1994; Sarat and Felstiner 1988); this work, however, focuses on the manner in which attorneys can activate legal discourse *on their own behalf.*

Whether and how the law is used by attorneys in the community, however, is dependent on the "reciprocal interaction between law, environment, and culture" (McEvoy 2005:434). In considering these interactions, the law can be defined very broadly; it is not simply the law on the books, but includes everyday interactions with employer policies or administrative agencies (McEvoy 2006). A person's surroundings, or environment, then generate conditions that will either encourage or discourage an individual to turn to the law. Both the law and environment interact with culture, or the meanings people create and employ regarding the law; culture is contextual and can vary across individuals, as well as depending on an individual's situation (McEvoy 2006). These three concepts work together, as well as work on one another, to produce an individual's response to a legal situation. To understand whether and how attorneys employ the law in challenging gender inequality, their understandings of the law, the environment of the Internet community, and the culture of the legal profession must all be considered—as well as how these constructs work in tandem.

This work does not seek to establish whether attorneys actually choose in their "offline" lives to sue or to pursue other means of asserting a claim. Rather, it examines the process by which an online community provides a forum in which individuals can come to recognize that they experienced a rights violation, assign blame for violating that right, and navigate the process of deciding whether to make a claim. Increasing research has been focused on examining the dispute process, rather than dispute outcomes (see e.g., Felstiner, Abel, and Sarat 1980–1981; Yngvesson 1993; Quinn 2000; Albiston 2005; Marshall 2005). Understanding this process is essential to gain insight into how and why some disputes come to fruition. Those disputes that manifest a public claim to right, either through formal litigation or otherwise, are those that are more likely to shape public opinion and legal outcomes. The subjects of disputes that fail to materialize into rights claims are, as a result, left stagnant with little opportunity for legal transformation. It becomes imperative to develop insight into the manner in which the dispute process produces public rights claims.

In exploring the manner in which the dispute process can develop in an online community, I first examine issues of the Internet environment in chapter 2. Chapter 2 describes the methods I employed in carrying out this research, in particular, the challenges and benefits of drawing data from an Internet community. I focus on the manner in which cybercommunication occurring in the environment of the online community can encourage or discourage counter-hegemonic discourse and reliance on the law. Chapter 3 then assesses the culture of the legal profession, analyzing the types of gender inequality faced by women in the legal practice. Findings from earlier research concerning gender discrimination in the legal profession paint a picture of the ways in which gender affects one's legal career and, consequently, the importance of identifying a remedy for gender inequality. In addition, the chapter analyzes discussions from the Internet community concerning gender issues; these analyses demonstrate that the Web site community serves as an outlet for attorneys to communicate on such topics, as well as the manner in which the experiences of online community members parallel those of subjects in earlier research. Further, chapter 3 examines some of the theories underlying discrimination, discussing the malleability of the concept of discrimination and the importance of a flexible notion of discrimination for this research.

Chapters 4, 5, and 6 address the concepts of both environment and law as generating important tools for interacting with and redressing the gender discrimination detailed in chapter 3. Chapter 4 focuses more specifically on the manner in which the community environment generates a space in which attorneys are able to progress through the dispute process. These online discussions have the capability of providing impetus to pursue some type of action against one's employer; at other times, responses of community members seem to discourage action. Nonetheless, the forum enables attorneys to anonymously challenge their employers' discriminatory practices, suggesting a powerful means of prompting change.

In chapters 5 and 6, I consider the role of the law, as well as its interactions with law firm culture and the Web site environment, in assessing the ability of law to generate change. Chapter 5 focuses on the role formal litigation might play in promoting change for women attorneys. Both the barriers that exist to success in formal litigation, as well as the manner in which attorneys in the Greedy Associates community discuss litigation, are explored. Finally, in chapter 6, I assess whether the law can serve as a useful tool for women attorneys, even if formal litigation is discouraged within the community. The use of legal discourse within the Internet community appears to be a powerful tool with the potential to challenge gender inequality and instigate change through appeals to legal rights.

Throughout this work, I seek to challenge the "myth of litigiousness" that surrounds lawyers, in particular the notion that lawyers possess special access to and knowledge of the legal system that allows them to manipulate it on their own behalf. Instead, I find that attorneys are equally, if not more, frustrated than laypersons in their attempts to challenge gender inequality through formal litigation. In addition, lawyers, despite their legal training, call upon both formal and *informal* notions of discrimination when confronted with circumstances colored with inequity. Consequently, attorneys use legal discourse to challenge situations that have been both recognized as prohibited employment practices, as well as actions that have yet to be so recognized. It is their ability and willingness to use legal discourse in this manner that gives it power to create change, because they offer new interpretations and understandings of gender discrimination that can prompt a rearticulation of one's conception of gender relationships and power.

It is online communication, however, that appears to present the greatest opportunity for employing legal discourse to challenge and alter gender. The anonymity provided by this forum provides the opportunity for attorneys to exercise power over their identities—to engage in exchanges that might not occur in an offline environment due to expectations regarding gender, or a sense of self-preservation regarding one's career. In addition, the Internet permits the flow of counterhegemonic discourse as it alters power relations, providing associate attorneys with a protected forum in which to challenge the actions of their employers. Through its nesting in a legal context, legal discourse becomes a natural resource for community participants. It is this discourse that lends legitimacy and strength to demands for gender equality and the development of new definitions of gender discrimination.

The power of Internet communities to effect change in our offline environments is likely to be a topic of growing focus over the coming years. Internet communities are increasingly used not only as a source of information or communication but also as a means to mobilize. As Gatson and Zweerink (2000:106) noted, "[o]ne of the reasons why concerns of the Internet as a communications technology have surfaced is its potential for influencing the development of human communities."

2

Methods—Exploring an Internet Community

The Method of Online Ethnography

The Internet has opened up a new realm of research opportunities for social scientists, both through the increased accessibility of databases and information sources and through the development of online communities that have created more easily accessible field research sites. As a result, a growing number of individuals are engaging in the practice of "cyber ethnography"—or "the study of humans in virtual communities and networked environments" (Mizrach n.d.). Cyber ethnographies focus on the idea that "the new... communities are no longer defined by geographic or even semiotic (ethnic/religious/linguistic) boundaries. Instead, communities are being constructed in cyberspace on the basis of common affiliative interests, transcending boundaries of class, nation, race, gender, and language" (Mizrach n.d.).[1] Visualizing an online community as an actual place where a social scientist can "observe, visit, stay and go," has prompted researchers in the field to query to what extent traditional ethnographic methods can be transplanted to the study of online communities (Jones 1999:17).

Traditional ethnographic methods rely on the notion that there is a particular community to be studied, to which an individual can be admitted, can be expelled, and for which there are particular guiding principles or laws. Communities need not have geographic boundaries, as individuals who share common interests can constitute a community, in addition to those who share a physical location (Fernback 1999). Some have questioned, however, whether online forums can be considered true communities, as individuals often move in and out of the forums at random; other individuals "lurk" in the forum, simply reading posts but not interacting with the members (Jones 1999). If people are able to quickly enter and leave the forum, are there any true community boundaries? Further, is there any community culture that can be maintained in such a rapid turnstile of an environment (Jones 1999)?

Many of those who have studied online forums have found that they do, in fact, constitute communities that permit the application of traditional ethnographic research principles. Fernback (1999) argues, however, that not every online interaction can establish a community; rather, the label of community must be reserved for places in which participants do more than share online discussions concerning common interests. To determine whether an online forum constitutes a community, one must interpret the site's "ideology, agency, power, ontology, roles, and boundaries," just as must be done in an offline gathering in assessing the presence of a community (Fernback 1999:216). In exploring some of these elements, Gatson and Zweerink (2000) determined that a fan-based Web site constituted a community due to practices such as (1) the presence of criteria for authentic group membership; (2) group members defining rules, or laws, that set forth the protocol for proper group interaction; (3) members engaging in the patrolling of the boundaries of the community to expel those who do not belong and/or who violate rules for proper behavior; and (4) engaging in political practices, such as encouraging members to unite for charitable causes or to promote the development of a diverse group membership in the community. As will become evident, similar types of practices have occurred in the online field site used for this research, rendering it appropriate for the use of ethnographic field research.

Due to the parallels between cyber communities and traditional communities, cyber communities can be studied in much the same manner as traditional communities, utilizing principles of ethnographic field research. The same practices, as well as the same concerns, applied in ethnographic field research must therefore be employed in the study of online communities. As noted by Fernback (1999:216), ethnographers in an online community must "attempt a measure of reflexivity, to separate oneself from the subjects being studied; they must develop a sense about the truthfulness and candor of their informants, just as ethnographers of the nonvirtual must; and they must use a theoretically informed framework for their research, just as ethnographers have traditionally done."

Thus, my study adapts the elements of traditional ethnographic field research to "a largely [or totally] unseen group of subjects" (Gatson and Zweerink 2000:107–108), who can be observed only through their disembodied online interactions. Specifically, I engaged in participant observation of the field site, employing ethnographic techniques to gain an understanding of the background of the participants, the content of the Web site, and the frequency of its use. During my period of observation, I never posted messages within the community, but participated as a "lurker" at the Web site—reading the message threads, without commenting. The findings of my participant observation are combined with content analysis of the messages posted to the Web site, to produce the research results. Details regarding content analysis and coding methods are contained in appendix 2.1.

The Greedy Associates Community: The Field Research Site and My Initial Forays

The message boards of the Web site www.greedyassociates. com serve as the site for this study's field research. The Greedy Associates Web site, copyrighted in 2000, is a "site dedicated to providing a forum for discussing issues concerning life as a lawyer" ("About Us," www.greedyassociates. com). The site contains a job board, resources for individuals seeking jobs or preparing to apply to law schools, legal research resources, and—most importantly for the purposes of this study—message boards addressing issues concerning law firm life and practice (see figure 2.1). The actual stated "goal" of the Web site community is to "provide Internet services such as an Internet 'public square' where people can discuss issues relating to the practice of law" ("Privacy Policy," www.greedyassociates.com).

The Greedy Associates message board is a threaded message board in which posts are organized by topic. An individual can create a new topic or reply to an old one. By clicking on the subject line of any message, one is brought to the content of that particular message, as well as to all messages that came before and after on the same subject line (see figure 2.2). Each message is also numbered in the order in which it was posted, beginning with the first message ever posted on the Web site as message number one. A search engine allows the user to search the message

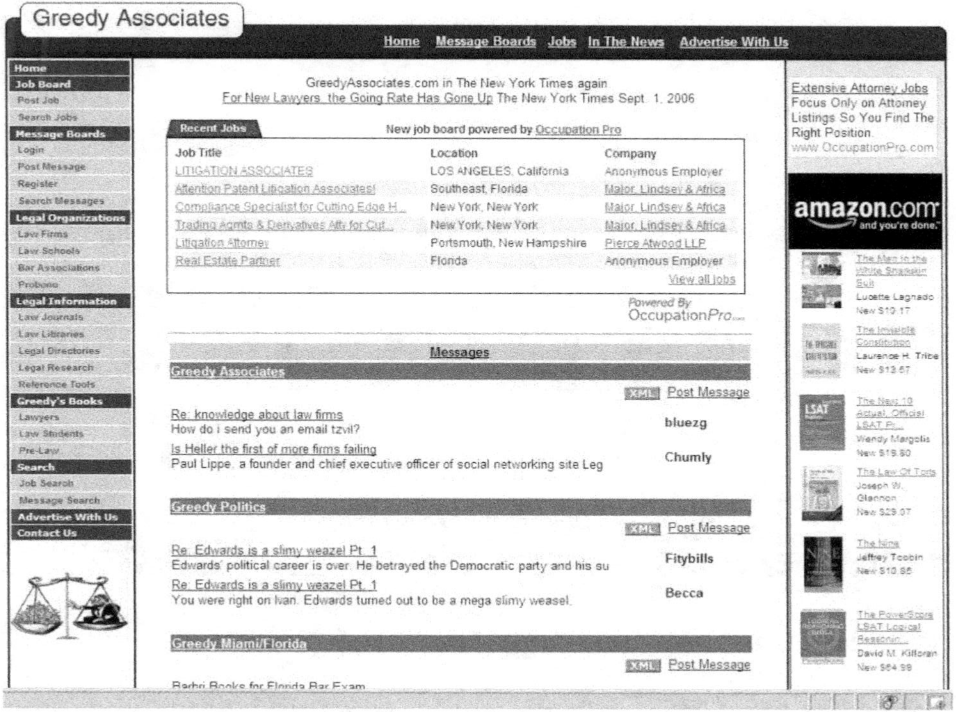

Figure 2.1 Home page.

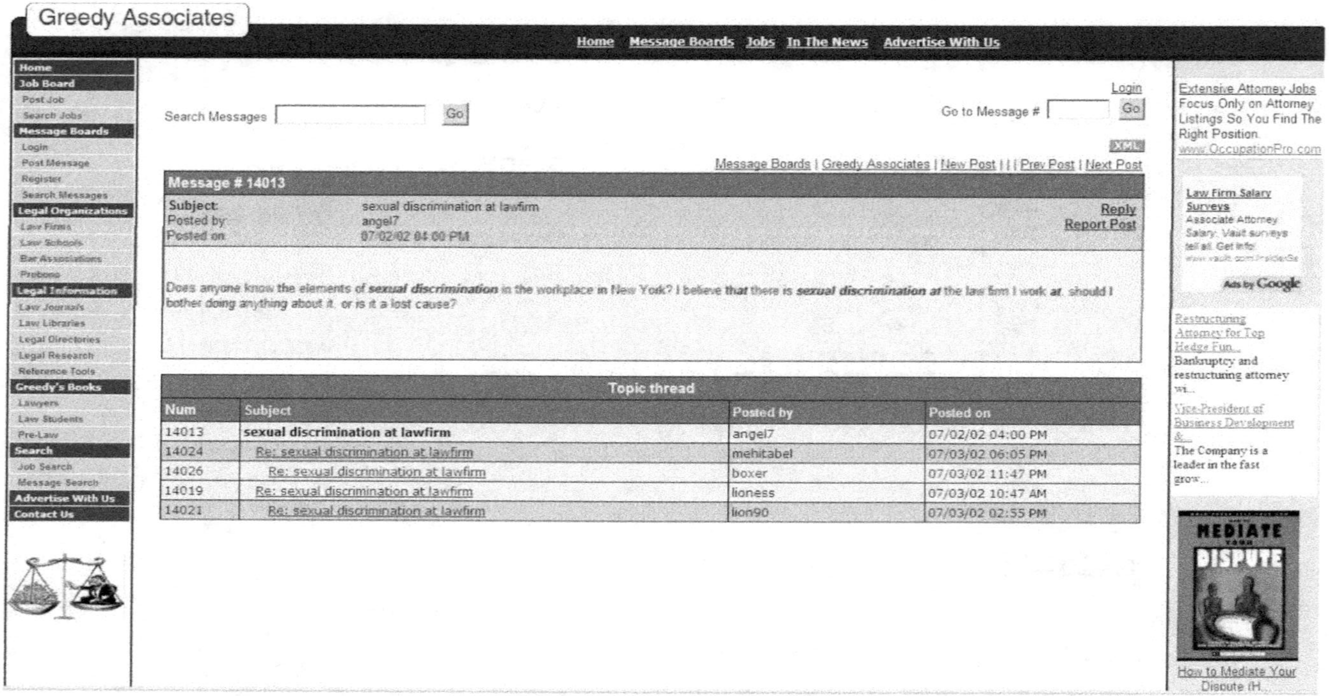

Figure 2.2 Message thread.

board for posts containing particular phrases or names, as well as to search by message number.

The messages themselves on the Greedy Associates board concern questions regarding firm salaries, billable hour requirements, and working environments. Both attorneys and law students utilize the message board in their hunt for an "ideal" legal position. Through the use of the message boards, individuals are able to anonymously post information about the firms for which they work, or wish to work. Visitors to the board are able to exchange knowledge regarding issues that are of concern in the employer selection process.

The Greedy Associates Web site was created in the year 1999,[2] a year marked by large salary raises for lawyers throughout much of the country. Law firms on the West Coast initiated these salary hikes, attributable in part to their success in representing Internet start-up companies. Once some firms began to offer salaries $30,000 to $50,000 or more over what other firms were offering to incoming attorneys, many other firms felt compelled to match these salary raises to compete for top candidates. The Internet was ablaze with rumors concerning which law firms might join suit with the West Coast firms in the salary wars. It was during this period that the Greedy Associates Web site was born. The Web site offered law students and attorneys a resource to obtain information concerning the status of the salary raises at firms throughout the country.

My Introduction to the Community

As a law student myself during this period, I was among those who visited the Web site to learn whether the firm where I would work post-graduation would join in (what was viewed by many as) the "insanity" of the huge salary raises. At the beginning of the third year of law school, the majority of law students decide about the law firm they intend to work for after graduation; the selected firm is typically one of the places for which the student clerked in the summer between second and third year. As a result, I had already accepted an offer from my firm when news of the salary increases began to spread throughout the legal community.

Discussions during breaks between classes were thick with whisperings about which firms would follow in the raises, with many of us citing to articles that tracked the income changes. It was during one of these discussions that a student mentioned the Greedy Associates Web site. Rather than waiting for the story to break in a news venue, he suggested, why not learn about firm salaries straight from current employees? The Greedy Associates page was full of salary information that was reported by attorneys employed by the firms; employees often learned of salary changes before the information was released to news outlets, and the Web site also reported salaries for smaller, less newsworthy firms.

We were all intrigued by the notion of having ready access to such "insider" information and, I assume, many of my fellow students reacted just as I did—by racing home and logging on. When I first accessed the Web site, it was much less developed than its current format. There was a list posted of "confirmed" salary information for particular law firms, with ranges from starting (first year) salaries to salaries for the more experienced attorney. In addition, there were messages posted with "breaking news" about new salary changes. I quickly searched for information about my firm and, disappointingly, came up with nothing concrete. I did, however, find messages asking for reports about my firm and I hoped that the information would surface. Consequently, I returned to the Web site periodically to check for updates and, at long last, found reported salaries for my firm (which were later confirmed by my employer). My focus during this period of use was on obtaining salary information, rather than other details about the legal practice; I did not access other messages posted on the Web site. I also did not post any messages to the Web site but, instead, "lurked" at the site—reading relevant messages, but not fully interacting in the community.

Following these excursions to the Greedy Associates Web site, I paid little attention to the community in the coming years. On occasion, I was directed to the Web site by colleagues to read about the latest law firm scandal, and I performed a cursory search a couple of times to determine whether any gossip was available about my own firm. During this period, I perhaps visited the Web site a dozen times and never posted a comment on the community boards. I noticed in passing that the Web site had developed substantially in content and appearance. The Web site was gradually taking on elements that made it more of a developed community, rather than simply a venue for salary information. When I eventually initiated this project in the early months of 2003, the Greedy Associates Web site was vastly more sophisticated than it was at my first visit in late 1999.

The Development of a Community

Despite its temporal connections with the 1999–2000 salary raises, the Greedy Associates Web site contains no history of the forces compelling the creation of the site, or the identification of its "webmasters." The first recorded message of the Greedy Associates community focused on obtaining information about job hunting in a particular market (GreedyEsq., 2, 8/20/1999).[3] Shortly thereafter, one individual (perhaps with some sarcasm) attempted to define the culture to prevail at the Web site, stating: "I'm greedy. Are you greedy? Only greedy people should be allowed to post here! ... This club is like way cool!" (*Latrell*, 19, 8/23/1999). Another attorney concurred, claiming "The board is cool. I hope that this board will be on topic and free of childish messages" (*Realga*, 23, 8/24/1999). And the board did stay "on topic" for a little over a month, focusing on information surrounding salaries, job hunts, and information about particular law firms.

The first message that strayed into a critique of the legal practice was then posted, asking attorneys about health problems associated with the legal practice (*Chas*, 121, 9/29/1999). There was no response to this post, but the board was increasingly home to messages that leaned toward an examination of complaints associated with the legal practice in general, or practice at a particular firm. These discussions have included addressing issues such as attitudes toward women or racial minorities, as well as working conditions. The transformation of an online forum from an informational source to a community focused on broader aspects of the members' lives is a common phenomenon. Sharf (1997) noted that a Listserv that originated primarily as an information source for individuals afflicted with breast cancer was subsequently transformed into a support group for breast cancer patients, survivors, and their families. Similarly, Gatson and Zweerink (2000) found that a Web site originally created for marketing and informational purposes for a television series later developed into a full-fledged community that focused not only on engaging in detailed analysis of the television show, but also on discussing the personal lives of its members, as well as larger political events.

Rheingold (1993:7) observed that such transformations are not uncommon in "computer-mediated communications...A continuing theme throughout the history of CMC [computer-mediated community] is the way people adapt technologies designed for one purpose to suit their own, very different, communication needs." The Greedy Associates community has certainly embraced this concept. Although the community originated to exchange salary information and other information concerning costs and benefits of employment at particular firms, the community members have transformed the forum to better accommodate their own requirements. Contrary to the usual depiction of attorneys as focused solely on the acquisition of wealth, as embodied in the Web site's self-deprecating name of "greedyassociates," the attorneys instead took control of the medium provided to them by the forum to express their viewpoints on a wide variety of issues relating to law firm life. At the Greedy Associates forum, the members discuss ethical dilemmas, discrimination, negotiating relationships in law firms, disillusionment with the legal practice, and wistful longings of finding a meaningful legal career or of leaving the practice altogether.

At times, their discussions deviate from the legal altogether, focusing instead on their personal problems or on political issues. The focus on the political, in fact, resulted in the creation of a separate forum, Greedy Politics, so as to isolate political talk from that concerned with the practice of law (although such talk still does surface at times on Greedy Associates). Similarly, other message boards have spun off on the Web site, including "Greedy Florida" and "Greedy London," two communities that parallel the content of the Greedy Associates community, but with a regional focus. The members of each of these boards "police" their boundaries to ensure that the community members are all present for a shared purpose. For instance, individuals introducing political analysis on the Greedy Associates board are frequently instructed by other board members to move their discussions to the Greedy Politics board. The creation of these separate boards demonstrates the way in which the needs of the community members played an active role in transforming the Web site and, eventually, altering the community and its members.

At the same time, however, the message board continues to fulfill its original purpose—to provide information about salaries and working conditions at particular firms to assist attorneys seeking new employment. In fact, days might go by during which messages focus solely on these issues, rather than on more inflammatory matters like discrimination or worker disputes. It is typically not long, though, before an individual introduces a topic unrelated to the hiring process and discussion of this matter is likely to dominate the board until it has been thoroughly explored. The community members, in this way, rely on the message board to provide basic information about the legal community, as well as to serve as a mechanism of support in navigating the challenges of legal practice.

Since its inception, Greedy Associates has grown to a sizeable community. A rough estimate of participants indicates that, if everyone accessing the Web site is an attorney, almost 3 percent of U.S. attorneys are exposed to the Web site each day.[4] It is important to note, however, that this figure is based on a daily population visiting the Web site. Not all visitors are repeat visitors, which means that the individuals who visit each day likely change to some degree. This would result in more attorneys being exposed to the Web site over time. Certainly, those visiting the

Web site are not representative of the population of U.S. attorneys. This work, however, involves an ethnography of an Internet community, rather than a representative analysis of the population of attorneys in the United States. Consequently, the lack of representativeness is not an issue for the purposes of this study. The question of who does participate in the community, however, is still pertinent; this is explored in greater detail in the following text.

Who Are the "Greedy Associates"?

Membership in the Greedy Associates community is, at first appearance, very open; this openness brings with it both benefits and challenges to the researcher. No action need be taken by individuals to have full access to peruse all of the messages of the Web site. Someone can, therefore, "lurk" at the Web site for an unlimited period of time, without ever revealing their presence or providing any information about themselves. If an individual wishes to post a message at the Web site, he or she can do so simply by registering as a new, anonymous user of the site and posting a response to an established message thread or generating a new one. The registration process consists of entering a user name, password, and a working e-mail address (see figure 2.3). The registrant is not required to provide any demographic information, such as gender, race, age, or geographic location. Further, the individual need not provide any information connected with his or her status in the legal community, such as whether he or she is in fact an attorney, an associate or partner, or his or her area of practice.

Once registered, an individual is free to post messages at the Web site. Messages can be posted in two ways: an individual can either respond to a message already posted

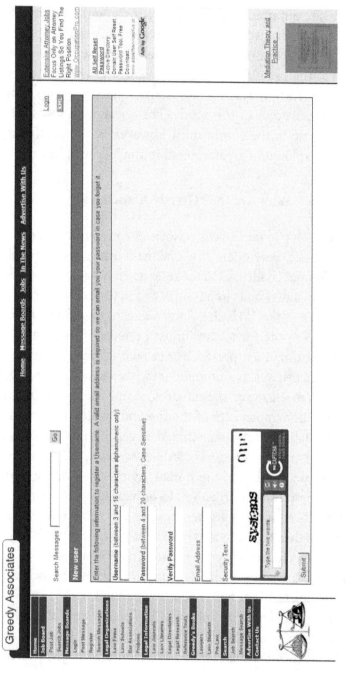

Figure 2.3 Registration.

on the Web site or can create a new topic thread. After selecting one of these options, the user is taken to a "Post a Message" screen, which requires the entry of the username, password, and the message itself (see figure 2.4). The message will be displayed on the board after it is posted, and others will immediately be able to view it and respond. This simple registration and posting process allows wide access to community participation, as compared with some Web sites that require the provision of detailed personal information and/or membership.

Individuals participating in the community in general, and responding to claims of discrimination specifically, come from a variety of law firms and types of practices. Demographics of individuals who participate in the community are, however, unavailable due to the limited information required during the registration process. Details regarding issues such as race, class, gender (detailed further, below), or practice type cannot be produced in describing "who are the Greedy Associates." Nonetheless, the lack of specific details regarding such characteristics should not affect the overall results of these analyses. The discourse occurring in the community is not necessarily representative of attorneys as a whole, and need not be. This research involves the examination of online communication to determine its utility in the dispute process, as well as its potential role in altering understandings of discrimination. Consequently, it is the discourse occurring in the community that is the focus of analysis, rather than demographics or perceived offline outcomes of the interactions. If some demographic categories or law firms are overrepresented, therefore, it is not particularly relevant to the major research questions of this work.[5]

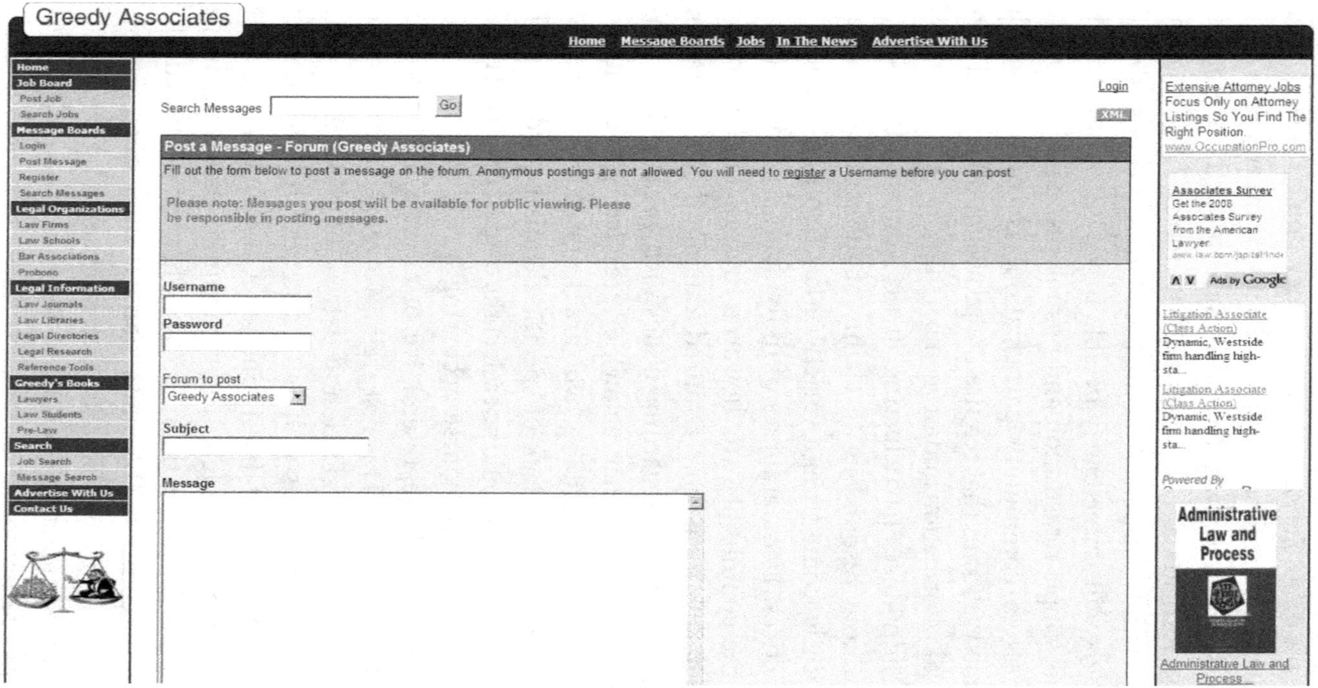
Greedy Associates
Home
Message Boards
Jobs
In The News
Advertise With Us
Home
Job Board
Post Job
Search Jobs
Message Boards
Login
Post Message
Register
Search Messages
Legal Organizations
Law Firms
Law Schools
Bar Associations
Probono
Legal Information
Law Journals
Law Libraries
Legal Directories
Legal Research
Reference Tools
Greedy's Books
Lawyers
Law Students
Pre-Law
Search
Job Search
Message Search
Advertise With Us
Contact Us
Search Messages
Go
Login
XML
Post a Message - Forum (Greedy Associates)
Fill out the form below to post a message on the forum. Anonymous postings are not allowed. You will need to register a Username before you can post.
Please note: Messages you post will be available for public viewing. Please be responsible in posting messages.
Username
Password
Forum to post
Greedy Associates
Subject
Message
Extensive Attorney Jobs
Focus Only on Attorney Listings So You Find The Right Position.
www.OccupationPro.com
Associates Survey
Get the 2008 Associates Survey from the American Lawyer
Ads by Google
Litigation Associate (Class Action)
Dynamic, Westside firm handling high-sta...
Litigation Associate (Class Action)
Dynamic, Westside firm handling high-sta...
Powered By
Administrative Law and Process
Administrative Law and Process...

Figure 2.4 Post a message.

The Gender Question

The secrecy surrounding the identity of the online participants and their characteristics posed some concern for this study. Ideally, when researching gender inequality in the legal practice, one would wish to know the gender of the individuals posting particular comments at the Web site. The gender of the participants would certainly be of interest in determining the number of women who participate in the forum and, thus, could be expected to be exposed to a movement occurring on the Web site. Further, the gender of community members could be relevant in examining the manner in which gender affects whether members value litigation as a means to address gender inequality, or whether men or women are more likely to use legal discourse in the community.

Ultimately, however, the gender of the community members is perhaps less important than might first be indicated. The gender of an individual who makes a particular post is less significant than the fact that the message has been publicized, and it will perhaps affect the actions of other community members and/or employers. For instance, assume one community member posts a message that describes a practice of gender discrimination in a particular law firm. The research questions raised by this post concern, primarily, what type of response the message receives both inside and outside of the community. Do other community members encourage litigation as a means to redress the harm? Do they use legal discourse to assert a right to a working environment free of discrimination? Do employers respond to the message by denying the practice of gender discrimination, or offering a remedy? In answering these questions, the gender of those responding is less pertinent than the fact that the discourse has entered the community and has prompted a response of some kind. Both men and women in the community are equally likely to be exposed to both the original post and the subsequent responses; those men and women might choose to respond online, and they might choose to refrain. The discourse, nonetheless, has the potential to affect their personal and work lives, regardless of their participation or their knowledge of the gender of the community members. As a result, the gender of the participants becomes less pertinent than the content of the interactions themselves.

Nonetheless, I have attempted to identify the gender of respondents throughout this work to provide some context for the responses. Warhol (1999:94) notes that a researcher may "only rely on posters' self-representation (and on self-perpetuating stereotypes of the masculine behavior of men and the feminine behavior of women) to draw conclusions about the sex of persons who write Internet messages." Consequently, if the individual self-identifies a gender, this gender was reported.[6] Further, a gender was reported if the individual's username reflects a strong indication of a particular gender (e.g., a name such as "HoustonLawGirl" would suggest a female identity). When individuals do not self-identify, I have attempted to determine gender through the analysis of various verbal cues. Although some studies indicate that there are particular online conversational styles that are characteristic of men and women, they also suggest that the community "culture" can influence the conversational style used by members (Kendall 2000; Warhol 1999; Sharf 1997; Baym 2000).[7] In other words, women might choose to use masculine styles in some communities, and men might employ feminine styles in others. As a result, it becomes difficult to identify the gender of an individual posting a message if the online community is dominated by one type of conversational style, since all community members, regardless of gender, might choose to adopt this style.

Observations to date indicate that the conversational style at the Greedy Associates Web site is not dominated by a "masculine" or "feminine" style; rather members generally express conversational styles that possess characteristics of each. This could provide some indication that there is a gender balance of sorts within the community that has not permitted one style to take hold. At the same time, however, there are potential obstacles to labeling an individual as male based simply on "conversational style" when one is studying a community based around a profession that is dominated by aggressive conversational styles. As a result, I have attempted to identify the gender of participants when the individuals have self-identified or when gender is readily discernable based on context; I have been more cautious in labeling individuals as male or female based simply on conversational style.

Employing the above-described techniques, I attempted to draw some conclusions concerning the gender breakdown of participants in the Greedy Associates community. I reviewed all posts made during the work week of February 28, 2005 through March 4, 2005. Of all of the messages posted to the community, approximately 47 percent of the authors could be identified as men, 25 percent as women, and 28 percent were undetermined (see table 2.1). This initial finding seems to suggest a dominance of men participating in the community. When individuals who make repeat posts are removed, however, 27 percent of the community participants were men, 24 percent women,

Table 2.1   Gender of community members posting during one week

Gender	Men (%)	Women (%)	Undetermined (%)
Total Posts	46.8	24.7	28.5
Individuals	27.3	24.2	48.5
Repeat Posters	61.4	25	13.6

and 48 percent undetermined. One can see that identifiable men comprise a much larger portion of individuals who make multiple posts during the week (61 percent), resulting in the total number of posts made by individuals identified as male being larger than that of those identified as female. Individuals with an undetermined gender comprised the greatest number of all individuals posting at the site, but these individuals were much less likely to make repeated posts. Consequently, individuals who can be identified as men do dominate the overall number of messages, but they do not seem to comprise a greater number of actual identifiable participants in the community.

The similarity between the percentages of individuals identified as men and as women parallels findings of other studies of online participation, where women were found to engage in online interactions in numbers either roughly similar to men, or in greater numbers (Ross et al. 2005; Gatson and Zweerink 2004a). At the same time, however, communities that are not focused on feminine issues are frequently dominated by men in terms of participation, as men might use their social power to control and dominate the interactions (Wasserman and Richmond-Abbott 2005). This could discourage repeated postings by women, resulting in women being more likely to "lurk," reading responses, but posting messages of their own less frequently.

Questions of Access

In addition to lacking information concerning the gender of the community members, the manner in which individuals register at the Web site results in a dearth of statistics concerning race, ethnicity, socioeconomic status, or political views. Even if such information was provided, Web site communities are unlikely to provide a representative sample of a population (Sharf 1997). On the one hand, anyone who has access to the Internet is free to join the community, which has the potential for resulting in a diverse mix of individuals; on the other hand, access is likely to be affected by demographic factors. Race, ethnicity, income, age, marital status, and language skills will all affect access in terms of both acquiring the necessary equipment, and the knowledge and skills to use the equipment (Wasserman and Richmond-Abbott 2005).[8] In China, this problem of access has stymied recent attempts to use the Internet to organize and challenge governmental practices, as those who are most likely to be harmed by government policies are the least likely to have access to the Internet (Gifford 2005).

The question of access is perhaps less problematic in the proposed research than in many studies dealing with Internet studies, however. Kendall (1999) observes that income and occupation are important factors in gaining access to online forums; in particular, having access to the Internet at work and the autonomy to use the Internet for personal activities is a significant concern, as well as having an income that would permit private Internet access at home. Since this research focuses on attorneys, both conditions are likely to be met. The majority of attorneys will have Internet access for their business, and the legal profession is a highly autonomous one in which most lawyers will be able to devote some work time to personal online activities. Further, attorneys largely fall into a higher socioeconomic status category that would permit them to have Internet access at home, and their job demands often require such access. In addition, as this research focuses primarily on the activities of associate attorneys, these individuals will be younger and likely more familiar and skilled in the use of computers and the Internet. Indeed, the majority of legal research nowadays occurs online, requiring associate attorneys to have strong technological skills.

A Theory of Cybercommunication: Altering Identity and Embracing Anonymity

Online communities possess many of the characteristics found in offline communities. Individuals in online communities often define group membership, patrol borders, develop laws and regulations, and encourage members to engage in political or social causes (see e.g., Gatson and Zweerink 2000; Fernback 1999). Nonetheless, online community interaction and communication possess a number of decidedly unique characteristics. Individuals exchange and respond to information in an atmosphere devoid of verifiable physical embodiment. This removal from one's physical body limits the available arsenal of communication tools and cues; one cannot rely on voice intonation or nonverbal cues to convey information (see e.g., Kendall 2002; Gatson and Zweerink 2002; appendix 2.1). At the same time, however, this liberation from one's physical self permits the exercise of power over identity, as well as over other individuals. It is this unique ability of online interactions to shift control over identity and social hierarchies that holds the most promise for adapting the Greedy Associates community to a forum for engaging in the dispute process and challenging inequalities.

Researchers examining interactions in cyberspace have observed that the disembodiment permitted in online communities allows for a greater freedom in self-identification. Kendall (2002) and O'Farrell and Vallone (1999), for instance, have noted that members in online communities sometimes choose to present themselves as a different gender or race than their offline identity. This freedom to perform a new identity permits flexibility in terms of conversational styles, sexual interactions, and other manifestations of gendered performance.

Consequently, gender (and other defining character-istics) gain fluidity in an online community, resulting in both the shoring up of, as well as the deconstruction of, traditional gender norms. Individuals can switch their gender identity, but they can also simply conform to an alternative gender performance with greater freedom than in an offline environment. This freedom can permit the exploration of alternative means of understanding and addressing situations and problems than might occur offline. Within the Greedy Associates community, there exists an opportunity for male and female attorneys to explore issues surrounding gender inequality with greater freedom and honesty than might be available offline. Members are able to draw upon the anonymity available in the community to express viewpoints that are perhaps contrary to those expected for their offline personalities— either due to their gender, or due to their position as an employee of a law firm. The potential for fluid identity is an essential element for seeking change and shaping new definitions of discrimination.

Even those who do not engage in gender switching in Internet communities, oftentimes find themselves in communities that demand adherence to a particular conversational style; this style might or might not be in agreement with their offline identity. Differing communication styles have been found to dominate male-dominated and female-dominated communities, for example. Kendall (2000, 2002) examined a community with a barlike atmosphere that is dominated by male members; she found that as a result of the overwhelmingly male presence at the Web site, both men and women in the community distanced themselves from femininity and from women in general. Men, regardless of their sexual orientation, were quick to employ banter that depicted women as sexual objects; in addition, the atmosphere on the Web site was frequently aggressive and the members spent a large portion of their time invoking their technical skills (a practice Kendall attributes to a new development in heterosexual masculine norms).

Although the Internet is traditionally viewed as a male realm, in which women must conform to masculinized discourse to participate, a number of researchers have found that when Web site communities center around "female" topics, the dynamic shifts. Their research suggests that, rather than women seeking to conform to a masculine communication style, it becomes the men who then conform to feminine conversational dynamics. For instance, Warhol (1999) explored a Web site devoted to the discussion of a soap opera, a subject perceived as a feminine habit. In this community, both male and female members engaged in a conversational style in keeping with what has been observed as characteristic of women; comments were typically met with support and agreement, disagreements were respectful, and emoticons were frequently employed to soften statements that could be taken in a harsh manner. Similarly, Baym (1995, 2000) examined a community centered on soap opera fans and found, as well, that the feminine subject matter served to color the dynamics of those participating in the community. Sharf (1997) observed similar conversational styles in her study of a breast cancer Web site community that was dominated by women, finding that the conversational style was very open and respectful; in fact, one male participant noted that he doubted whether male cancer patients would engage in such an open exchange concerning sexual problems associated with their disease.[9]

It is logical to assume that other conversational styles, beyond gendered ones, play a similar role in influencing the types of interactions that occur in the community. The Greedy Associates community is dominated by attorneys and, as such, legal language is bound to surface more than in other environments. Just as men visiting a female-dominated community might be more apt to take a respectful tone with other participants (Warhol 1999; Sharf 1997), attorneys participating in a community such as Greedy Associates are more likely to employ legal language than they would in other contexts. Consequently, it becomes more probable (as examined in chapter 6) that these attorneys would rely on legal discourse and a reference to legal rights when discussing inequality than if such discussions were occurring in a community that was not identified with the legal community.

Online communities not only offer the opportunity for power over one's own identity, but they also hold promise for exerting power over others, thereby altering power relations. The Internet has the capacity to create counterhegemonic discourse, "challenging established systems of domination and legitimizing and publicizing political claims by the powerless and marginalized" (Warf and Grimes 1997:260). This possibility becomes particularly significant for individuals who are unable to openly articulate their demands offline (Warf and Grimes 1997).

Indeed, the Internet has been used by employees for this very purpose. University professors in Israel employed computerized messaging to organize a nationwide strike (Pliskin and Romm 1994). Similarly, union activists and labor organizers are able to use the Internet to "denounce irresponsible corporations or to announce their own efforts to curtail them" (Warf and Grimes 1997:265). The potential for this type of activity results in management "fear[ing]" that [computer networks] will threaten control by accelerating the flow of (mis)information, including rumors, complaints, jokes, and subversive communications" (Wellman et al. 1996:226, citing Finholt and Sproull 1990). In one large corporation, women organized a computerized conference to discuss their careers; in response, management monitored the conversation due to fear of demands for unionization or affirmative action (Zuboff 1988). These fears compelled one corporation to go so far as to shut down a company-sponsored "Gripenet" when the employees began to use this medium to challenge corporate practices (Emmett 1982). The anonymity and organizational capacity of online communities offers the opportunity to engage in communications that confront the dominant discourse and subvert preexisting power relations. In the Greedy Associates community, associate attorneys are then presented with a unique opportunity to alter the power structure and challenge employers concerning gender inequality.

The structure of the Greedy Associates community supports a level of anonymity that permits both fluid self-identity and counterhegemonic discourse. The limited requirements for accessing the Greedy Associates community allow for a great deal of anonymity connected with participation in the community, despite its public nature. The Web site has a detailed privacy policy that states that the identity of individuals posting at the site will remain confidential in the absence of any good faith belief of a legal obligation to disclose such information. Perhaps because of this policy, members enjoy a certain sense of anonymity as to their offline identities. Less than two weeks after the creation of the Web site, this assumption of anonymity was first addressed, with one attorney informing another: "As far as your detective work goes, I have nothing to fear, even if you do know who I am, which is totally impossible" (*Skekemebaby*, 64, 9/06/1999). The belief of anonymity is evident in this individual's assertion that knowledge of his or her identity is "totally impossible."

Nonetheless, Greedy Associates' participants remain understandably reticent to provide background information about themselves due to the public nature of the forum. For instance, disclosing information regarding an individual's employer, the city in which he or she works, or the practice group in which he or she works could be sufficient to identify the individual depending on the size of the person's law firm. Some community members, however, are less careful about such issues and at least one individual was openly identified by a former coworker due to the information revealed on the site (*gyroyeero*, 11173, 2/21/02). The other Web site participants rallied around the "outed" poster, chastising the individual who revealed the poster's identity. One male attorney responded incredulously to another who identified the individual, stating: "I can't believe you have the time to try to figure out who is making statements on this and other boards and violate their anonymity. Just because you don't agree with someone who has probably been royally screwed by the firm doesn't give you a license to expose them to the world" (*shearman suks*, 11245, 2/23/02). The existence of the Web site relies on the ability of individuals to engage in anonymous discussions without endangering jobs or well-being; thus revealing poster identities is considered unacceptable. As explored in chapters 3 and 5, it is this anonymity that provides the opportunity for altering gender relations in the legal profession.

Appendix 2.1

Methodology

Researching Online versus Offline
Earlier research examining gender inequality in the legal practice has relied on interviews, surveys, or direct observation. In contrast to interviews or observation, drawing on data from a Web site community can present a number of difficulties. Online exchanges pose challenges in terms of understanding nuances that are normally communicated through expressions, tone of voice, or body language. More difficulties are presented in discerning emotions, such as sarcasm or teasing, in an online dialogue. These challenges dissipate the longer one spends within a community, however, as the researcher becomes familiar with the personalities of particular community members and is able to differentiate between expressions of sarcasm, teasing, anger, or sympathy. Indeed, Kendall (1999) notes that

a social scientist cannot engage in research involving an Internet community without spending adequate time in the community to familiarize oneself with regulars; brief visits to solicit responses to surveys constitute irresponsible research.

Further, Sharf (1997) notes that the lack of visual or tactile contact with other community members can actually prove a benefit in that community members might be more uninhibited in an Internet environment where the interaction does not occur face-to-face; this lack of inhibition can result both in the exposure of information that might not otherwise be revealed, as well as in some individuals discussing issues in a less formal, and perhaps more emotional way than would occur in a face-to-face interaction. As a result, the researcher might glean a more rich, and full data source than would be available from interviews or direct observation. Finally, Gatson and Zweerink (2004a) note that the disembodied interaction associated with the Internet can also prove advantageous for both the researcher and the community members, in that it allows individuals to deliberate carefully over their responses, should they so choose. Accordingly, subjects' responses might be more carefully considered than those received in other formats, both in content and in tone.

Reliance on an Internet community as a research site can also be problematic in that the sample is necessarily a self-selected one. This problem differs from that of access, as many individuals who have access to the Internet will not choose to visit the Greedy Associates community or to become community members. Perhaps only those women attorneys who feel particularly wronged, for instance, will choose to participate in the community; if this is the case, then the experiences expressed by women attorneys at the

Web site will not be representative of women attorneys as a whole.[10] This study, however, does not seek to determine whether the types of experiences addressed in the community are representative of all women attorneys. Instead, I am examining the manner in which the discourse in the community concerning gender inequality or harassment could serve as a means to challenge inequalities. As a result, whether the types of complaints made in the community are indicative of systemic problems is less relevant than the ability of the community to provide a forum to challenge inequality, perhaps prompting employer response and/or other women to challenge inequality in a similar manner.

Participation in the Web site can also be very time consuming, as noted by Sharf (1997); if an individual wishes to be immersed in the community and to keep up with all messages posted on a single day, he or she might devote multiple hours to the task of reading and posting each day. For any individual, this would be an imposing task, but for an attorney whose every quarter hour must be accounted for to maintain his or her billable hours' demands, the time requirements of the community might serve to exclude some individuals from full participation. Due to the nature of the Web site community, however, an individual is able to access the community at all hours of the day; community members can therefore find support at their fingertips even in the midnight hours (Sharf 1997). As a result, attorneys who might be unable to access the Web site during the day might find the time outside of work hours rendering this barrier less imposing.

Although access issues, coupled with self-selection, are likely to result in a sample of individuals that is not representative of attorneys as a whole, the Web site community also allows interaction to occur among a range of individuals who might not otherwise interact and to whom the researcher might not otherwise have access. Individuals from a variety of geographic locations are able to visit the Web site community and to interact with others around the country, as well as around the world. Further, they are exposed to individuals with a wide range of experiences and expertise. For the community members, this increases the likelihood of interacting with individuals who have a shared experience (Sharf 1997); for the researcher, this results in an increased sample of individuals corroborating shared experiences, confirming that such events are not isolated occurrences.

Size of the Greedy Associates Community

Alexa is a Web information service developed by www.amazon.com that provides a search and data toolbar to its users and, in return, collects information about Internet traffic and use from those who employ its toolbar. As part of its analysis of Internet traffic, Alexa developed a measure of "reach" for Web sites that ascertains the number of users of the site; reach can be "expressed as the percentage of all Internet users who visit a given site" (www.alexa.com). The three month average reach for the greedyassociates.com Web site for October 2004 was 2.8 percent; this is the average of the daily reach figures over a three month period and means that if random samples of one million Internet users were taken, one would find on average that 28,000 of them visit www.greedyassociates.com on a given day.

According to the American Bar Association, there were 1,084,504 resident and active attorneys in the United States in 2004. If all individuals who visit the Greedy Associates

Web site are attorneys (which is certainly not the case), and all are U.S. citizens (which, again, is not the case), the largest population of U.S. attorneys who are accessing the Web site each day according to Alexa's reach statistics would be approximately 2.6 percent (28,000/1,084,504) of all attorneys. Since law students, individuals not affiliated with the law, and non-U.S. citizens visit the Web site, this percentage is undoubtedly inflated; thus, best available estimates indicate that less than 2.6 percent of U.S. attorneys visit the Greedy Associates Web site each day. It is important to note, however, that this figure is based on a daily population visiting the Web site. Not all visitors are repeat visitors, which means that the individuals who visit each day likely change to some degree. This would result in more attorneys being exposed to the Web site over time.

Associated Ethical Concerns
Finally, ethical implications are raised in connection with using a Web site community as a research site. Clearly, there are benefits associated with conducting research in a Web site community, as the research is neither intrusive nor costly (Sharf 1999). Further, communications can be easily recorded, recalled at a later date, and preserved in either hard copy or electronic format. Concerns have been raised by some researchers, however, as to whether anonymity or confidentiality implications attach to the identity of the Web site, or to the communications themselves, as both appear in a public forum (Sharf 1999; Gatson and Zweerink 2004a, 2004b).

Researchers turning to Internet communities as their field sites have awarded varying levels of confidentiality and anonymity to their subjects. Kendall (2000), for example, assigned a fictitious name to the Web site community and to all of the members whom she cited. Other Web site communities have been assigned easily deciphered pseudonyms, or have been called by their actual online names (Gatson and Zweerink 2004a, 2004b). Gatson and Zweerink (2004a, 2004b), for example, opted to reveal the identity of the Web site community that was the subject of their research due to the impracticability of concealing the Web site's identity because of its ties to a popular television show, as well as the media attention that the community already received.

In addition to considering whether to reveal the Web site's identity, questions concerning the ownership of the communications themselves have also been raised. Some argue that as the communications are made on the Internet and are accessible by the public, the individuals have lost all rights associated with the communications (see, e.g., the viewpoint expressed by community members in Gatson and Zweerink 2004b). One perspective expressed by online participants is that when communications are made in the public Web site forum, those making the communications have rendered them up to the public discourse; if the conversation moves out of the Web site community and to e-mail or instant messaging, however, many individuals express an expectation of privacy (Gatson and Zweerink 2004b). Others contend that the anonymity that is associated with the Internet results in individuals revealing information that they might otherwise keep confidential; as a result, if a researcher appropriates the information without the individual's consent, ethical implications are raised (Sharf 1999). Sharf (1999:252) has noted that online discussion groups should perhaps contain warnings indicating that "postings are public statements subject to widespread accessibility." She cautions, nonetheless, that all of the burden should not be placed on the participant, and thus encourages the researcher to obtain informed consent from participants in a Web site community before using their communications in publications.

The Greedy Associates Web site contains a number of warnings cautioning its users concerning the public nature of their communications. In the "Terms of Use," the user is clearly instructed "You acknowledge that all Message Board postings are public and not private communications" (Terms of Use II.E., www.greedyassociates.com). Further, the user is emphatically informed (in all capital letters) that "your confidential use of this site cannot be guaranteed by us. We shall not be responsible for any harm that you or any person may suffer as a result of a breach of confidentiality in respect to your use of this site" (Terms of Use III, www.greedyassociates.com). The Web site also includes a separate "Privacy Policy." This policy cautions, "Please note that when you disclose personal information online such information can be collected and used by others." Finally, and perhaps most blatantly, when community members elect to post a message, the message entry block is headlined, in red, by the following: "Please note: Messages you post will be available for public viewing. Please be responsible in posting messages" (see figure 2.4).

The community members are, therefore, repeatedly instructed that their use of the Web site is not private or confidential, and that their communications thereon are public. Further, the Web site is frequently a news source for the media concerning events in the legal community; as a result, many online participants are aware that their communications are public and can and will be cited by outside sources. When community members of other Web sites have been aware of media attention, they have expressed a similar lack of expectation of privacy, due in part to their realization that journalists were free to frequent the Web site in search of quotes (Gatson and Zweerink 2004a, 2004b).

Nonetheless, one could argue that the online members whose quotes I chose to use in this work could be contacted to ensure their consent, as suggested by Sharf (1999). The difficulty in doing so, however, is that neither individuals' e-mail addresses are posted at the Web site, nor is there a link from the username to the e-mail address. As a result, there is no way to contact the individual privately to request informed consent. The only way to obtain informed consent, therefore, would be to post a public message to the forum, listing usernames and requesting contact. This could be problematic, as some individuals cited might no longer be frequenting the community; as a result, they might not view the message to provide consent. In addition, posting a public message could disrupt the field site and affect the activities of its members. This research was approved by a university Internal Review Board without a provision for obtaining informed consent from the online participants. Given the notice provided to the participants concerning the public nature of the forum, as well as the difficulties posed in contacting individual participants to obtain consent, informed consent was not sought in this particular study.

Content Analysis
In addition to the field study of the Greedy Associates community, I also conducted content analysis of the messages posted by community members. The messages examined were selected from those created between the dates of August 1999 (when the board was created) and March 2005; from the creation of the Web site through

October 24, 2004, members of the Web site community had posted 21,940 messages to the Greedy Associates board.

To engage in content analysis of the messages, I went through the typical steps of operationalizing my key variables, selecting posts using the search tool made available at the Web site, and coding data according to the categories I constructed to measure my key variables. For example, in the first portion of my study I examined ways that women are treated unequally from men in the legal practice; obviously, unequal treatment occurs on a number of levels. As a result, I operationalized my key variable of unequal treatment by formulating a list of types of unequal treatment that individuals might discuss in the Web site community.

Drawing on personal knowledge and a review of the literature, I compiled an extensive list of types of unequal treatment on the basis of gender in the legal community. These included categories such as comments about or that constituted sexual harassment; comments relating to gaining access to the "partnership gossip network" including engaging in sports spectatorship, disparaging colleagues, and consumption of alcohol; receiving unequal assignments; complaints concerning maternity leave; comments concerning women having to dress or act in a feminine manner; comments regarding women using their femininity to acquire assignments or promotions; and so on. I then selected posts from the time of the founding of the Web site in 2000 through March 2005 that fell into these categories, employing the search tool made available at the Web site for searching Web site messages. Finally, I coded the collected Web site messages in light of the constructed categories and analyzed my data to discuss gender inequality in the legal practice. This process was repeated for the content analysis in the subsequent sections of this book.

3

Gender Inequality in
the Legal Practice

Throughout this book, I examine both the manner in which community members respond to claims of discrimination made in the online community, as well as the means they propose to redress discrimination. Before exploring the means by which the community can assist in the development of disputes, however, a picture must be painted of the types of discriminatory behaviors faced by women and why they should be challenged. This chapter undertakes this task, examining findings from past research[1] that reveal the opposition women attorneys face to full entry into the legal practice.

In discussing these findings, I also present data reflecting gender discrimination as expressed by members of the Greedy Associates community. These data provide a number of beneficial insights. First, they reveal the types of discriminatory practices that members of the community find problematic in their everyday practices as attorneys. While surveys and interviews might result in reflection on objectionable behavior, and consequently a listing of practices that seem to discriminate, an examination of data in the Web site community reveals the practices that prompt attorneys to seek assistance or comment from other attorneys within the community. Such an examination sheds light on the discriminatory practices for which attorneys might be prepared *to seek redress*. Further, to the extent that reports of discrimination in the Internet community coincide with conduct reported through interviews and surveys, these correlations lend strength to the validity of the Web site community as a source for examining gender discrimination in the legal practice. In other words, if similar conduct is reported in this venue, it supports the notion that the Web site community is not simply a venue for expressing unusual grievances, which are unrepresentative of the experiences of women attorneys as a whole.[2] Once again, however, I must stress that the intent is not to provide a representative picture of discrimination in law firms. Instead, this chapter seeks merely to describe gender discrimination highlighted by other researchers, and to provide glimpses into the type of discourse surrounding gender discrimination that occurs in the Web site community.

Theoretical Background

What Is "Discrimination"?: Legal and Sociological Concepts Used in This Work

Throughout this book, I describe gender inequality in the legal practice and discuss means of using the law to challenge existing inequalities. In doing so, the notion of "discrimination" is either implicitly or explicitly present in my discussions of inequality, work done by prior researchers, and the way that members of the Greedy Associates community discuss inequality. It is useful, therefore, to provide a framework for understanding what is meant by discrimination in the context of this work, as its nesting in the law and society literature might prompt an assumption of a narrow, legalistic definition of discrimination. Discrimination, however, remains a very fluid concept, despite a wealth of literature from varying disciplines that has attempted to provide the term with a concrete definition (Baumle and Fossett 2005). This fluidity is mirrored in the way that courts, lawyers, sociologists, politicians, and various other laypersons discuss discrimination, and it is this definitional malleability that imbues the notion of discrimination with a great deal of power for prompting change. If what constitutes discrimination cannot be definitively set forth, then it is constantly vulnerable to challenges and rearticulation, serving as a powerful linguistic tool for change.

Sociologists have offered a range of definitions of discrimination that differ in the extent to which they identify characteristics of the discriminator, specify the intent of the discriminator, require a motivation for discrimination, specify groups or categories subject to discrimination, or require a particular outcome of discrimination (whether it is positive or negative). Levin and Levin (1982:51), for instance, suggest that discrimination consists of "differential or unequal treatment of the members of some group or category on the basis of their group membership rather than on the basis of their individual qualities." This definition does not require that the discriminator be motivated by prejudice or negative affect; instead, the discriminator could be motivated by group interest. In addition, the definition does not provide any guidance as to the type of group that can be the object of discrimination; the group could be a racial minority or majority, or it could also be individuals who graduated from a particular institution. One can see, therefore, that this definition is very general if it is applied strictly as stated; one would assume that Levin and Levin intended for the definition to cover differential treatment on the basis of an ascribed characteristic, although it is not specifically indicated.

Feagin and Eckberg (1980), on the other hand, have provided a definition of discrimination that is much more narrowly tailored. They contend that discrimination consists of "practices and actions of dominant race-ethnic groups that have a differential and negative impact on subordinate race-ethnic groups" (Feagin and Eckberg 1980:9). This definition, unlike Levin and Levin's, clearly intends to identify actions as discriminatory only if they are taken by dominant race and ethnic groups against minority groups. They specify only that the actions must have a negative impact on minority groups, regardless of the intent of the actors. Thus, Feagin and Eckberg's definition stands in stark contrast to Levin and Levin's in that it identifies a clear "bad actor"—majority race and ethnic groups. In addition, actions taken by minority groups against majority groups apparently would not be considered discrimination under Feagin and Eckberg's definition, regardless of negative outcome or intent.

These two sociological definitions of discrimination highlight some of the lack of consensus for a clear definition of discrimination existing within just the sociological literature. As mentioned previously, definitions vary as well in other disciplines (Baumle and Fossett 2005). A number of reasons could contribute to the lack of consensus concerning a single definition of discrimination. The overarching reason is likely attributable to the fact that viewing an act as discriminatory will differ according to race, gender, socioeconomic background, and political motivations. Further, power differentials will determine whose definition of discrimination gains dominance within the legal system. One can see simply by examining Feagin and Eckberg's definition of discrimination that definitions of discrimination can be strongly influenced by political or academic designs. Defining discrimination as existing only in actions taken by a member of a majority racial group against a minority racial group does not incorporate the fact that race discrimination can occur in the reverse situation, as well as within a racial group (see, for instance, instances in which African Americans of a darker phenotype have asserted discrimination by those of lighter skin). In addition, Feagin and Eckberg's definition does not acknowledge discrimination on the basis of gender, age, disability, or other protected classes. Thus, the definition advanced by Feagin and Eckberg appears to be advanced for a particular purpose, rather than as a broad definition of the practice of discrimination.

Within the legal system itself, individuals also advocate varying interpretations of the concept of discrimination. Most laypersons would likely expect that statutes prohibiting discrimination, such as Title VII of the Civil Rights Act of 1964, would contain a precise definition of what constitutes discrimination. This is not the case, however. Title VII prohibits employment decisions based on certain group characteristics, including race, color, religion, sex, and national origin (Title VII, Sec. 703[a]). It further identifies some specific discriminatory acts, such as failing to hire, promote, or increase the wages of an individual because of membership in a protected group (Title VII, Sec. 703[a]). After this general list of prohibited acts, Title VII includes vague language noting that it will be unlawful "otherwise to discriminate;" the statute fails, however, to set forth a specific definition of what it means to discriminate. The lack of a specific definition is undoubtedly attributable in large part to the difficulty in operationalizing an acceptable, encompassing definition of what it means to discriminate (as highlighted in the earlier discussion of sociological definitions of discrimination). Consequently, it has been left to lawyers and judges to shape the meaning of "discrimination," with differing perspectives vying for ratification.

For instance, as detailed in chapter 5, many contend that the definition of discrimination that has prevailed in sex discrimination decisions has been dictated by the male-dominated judicial system (MacKinnon 1979; Nelson and Bridges 1999; Baer 1999). Nelson and Bridges (1999) note that the concept of comparable worth failed as a result of the judicial system accepting the unsubstantiated evidence that the market, rather than discrimination, determines pay differences between men and women. By embracing this perspective, the court accepted the definition of discrimination (or lack thereof) that was advanced by the male-dominated bureaucracy. In this manner, courts began to place barriers on what types of so-called structural inequalities fall under the definitional umbrella of "discrimination." Similarly, MacKinnon (1979) and Baer (1999) note that the burden of what constitutes sexual harassment has been very difficult to meet for women due in large part to the fact that white men have been in the position to define what constitutes "discrimination" in these cases. As a result, women find that many situations that create seemingly intolerable working environments are not considered "discrimination" or "harassment" under the law. All of these factors indicate that discrimination definitions differ in part based on who is in power to render the final decision concerning the definition, whose interests will be protected by the definition, and the race, gender, and class of those individuals. Consequently, throughout this work the definition of discrimination is very much determined by the context in which it is discussed, as well as the characteristics of the individual invoking its use. At times, discrimination refers to actions that could potentially be actionable under state or federal law. But discrimination, as has been discussed, is broader than what has been recognized by the judicial system (McEvoy 2005). In fact, Title VII itself is quite broad in setting forth what constitutes discrimination, and it is only judicial interpretation of the statute that has narrowly curtailed rights under this law. As a result, what constitutes actionable gender inequality under the statute perhaps exceeds what has been currently recognized by the courts. Further, what attorneys recognize as being unfair workplace practices clearly exceeds what has been recognized under the law. As will be highlighted in chapter 5, although attorneys might look to the law in raising objections to workplace behavior, they frequently move beyond recognized prohibited behavior. They employ legal discourse to step outside of the formally recognized definition of discrimination and, thereby, implicitly suggest its rearticulation (Omi and Winant 1994; Bourdieu and Thompson 1991). The ability to both work within recognized definitions of gender discrimination, and to push those boundaries, is thus explored throughout this work. It is important, however, to bear in mind that attorneys, like laypersons, invoke idealistic notions of discrimination that are perhaps more comparable to Levin and Levin's broad sociological notion of discrimination, than the courts' narrow interpretations of gender discrimination.

Discrimination and Inequality in the Legal Practice

Although women now make up approximately half of those enrolled in law schools, they continue to face barriers in both admission to the profession, and in reaching high ranking positions (see table 3.1). In the year 2000, the American Bar Association reported that more than 70 percent of all attorneys are male, leaving the profession undoubtedly male-dominated (Rhode 2001; table 3.1). Further, more than 85 percent of federal judges are male, providing a decidedly male perspective to the interpretation of the law. Approximately 85 percent of all law firm partners are also male, and 95 percent of all managing partners (those with ultimate authority within a firm) are male. Notably, studies have found that men are approximately twice as likely to obtain partnership status as similarly qualified women (Rhode 2001), indicating that this disparity cannot be attributed simply to a lag due to women's delayed entry to the field. As a result, although there has been a narrowing of the gender gap between men and women in the profession, the legal profession remains a decidedly male one.

Table 3.1   Percentage of women and men in legal occupations, 2000

Occupation	Law Students	Attorneys	Partners	Managing Partners	General Counsels	Judges
Women	45	30	15	5	10	15
Men	55	70	85	95	90	85

A variety of theories have been suggested to explain the predominance of men in the law firm environment, both in numbers and in level of success. These theories include notions of discrimination and the exclusion of female attorneys by the male population, as well as the idea that women's choices result in a lower level of participation and success in the legal community. Theorists who attribute women's lesser participation and success in law to choice tend to argue that either women choose not to enter the profession in the first place or, once in the profession, they exclude themselves from the paths that lead to success.

The human capital theory, for instance, postulates that women are prevented entry into some occupations because they do not have the requisite skills, education, and/or desire to limit time spent on family demands (Reskin and Padavic 1994; Sokoloff 1992; Goldin 1990; Gerson 1985). Failure to possess the appropriate skills or the desire to sacrifice family for work is thus thought to impede entry and/or success in particular occupations. Critics of this theory cite studies showing that single women are just as likely as married women to work in female-dominated fields, suggesting weaknesses in the notion that women place family over work (see e.g., Reskin and Padavic 1994). Further, even if a woman planned to leave the labor force at some point due to family demands, she would make more money working in a male-dominated field; in addition, she gains little flexibility by working in a female-dominated field, as many so-called women's jobs (with the exception of primary and secondary school teaching) have not been found to be compatible with family demands. Finally, studies have found that predominantly male and female occupations require similar levels of education and skills, and that women exert as much effort and, on average, are considered as committed as men to their jobs (Reskin and Padavic 1994). As a result, arguments that skills differences or variations in work ethic limit women's entry or success in particular occupations seem unfounded.

Gender socialization theory also attributes inequality within occupations to choices made by women themselves, rather than to exclusion by others. Proponents of this theory argue that socially created "gender differences in values, interests, and thought processes" influence a woman's choice of occupation, as well as the specialty within that occupation, resulting in women choosing occupations and settings that are "gender-appropriate" (Hull and Nelson 2000:232; Betz and O'Connell 1989; Marini and Brinton 1984; Marini, Fan, and Finley 1996). Gender socialization is similar to the concept of sex-typed professions, discussed in the following text, but focuses on the idea of women choosing to exclude themselves from the profession because socialization creates a preference for different kinds of work for women and teaches women only the skills needed in the occupations deemed typical for women (Reskin and Padavic 1994; Gerson 1985). Gender socialization thereby perpetuates the existing boundaries between male and female jobs because it results in women not obtaining "skills and information relevant to male-dominated jobs"; as a result, women are either excluded from traditionally male jobs or not prepared for such occupations (Hull and Nelson 2000:233). Many criticize the gender socialization theory, arguing that women move back and forth between male-dominated and female-dominated jobs; if they are socialized to favor one over the other, this would not likely be the case (Reskin and Padavic 1994). Further, studies have indicated that career desires at youth rarely impact later career choices, which weakens the notion that early socialization affects later career choice (Gerson 1985).

In contrast to theories of human capital and gender socialization, other theories attribute women's lower levels of participation and success in law to actions taken by others, that is, to discrimination (Reskin and Padavic 1994; Sokoloff 1992; Goldin 1990; Epstein 1970). One of these theories which suggests that female exclusion is attributable to deliberate exclusion, rather than choice, is that of the sex-typed occupation (Epstein 1970). Professions share many characteristics of communities in that they are typically homogenous and exhibit shared norms and values. As a result, occupations typed as male or female are resistant to the attempted entry of members of the opposite sex into the profession. Epstein (1970:969) observes that women attempting to enter the legal profession find it difficult to gain access to "the exclusive society, to participate in its informal interactions, to understand the unstated norms, and to be included in the casual exchanges" due to their gender.

Women who do seek entrance into occupations sex-typed as male are often viewed as deviants and, as a result, are subject to social sanctions (Gerson 1985; Epstein 1970). A variety of studies have found that "sexist behavior is most likely to occur where organizational culture specifically values characteristics traditionally attributed to men and where power is supported by instrumental and social cliques" (Rosenberg, Perlstadt, and Phillips 1993:417; Acker 1990; Hearn and Parkin 1987; U.S. Merit Systems and Protection Board 1988). Thus, women entering into the legal profession—a field in which the "organizational culture…values characteristics traditionally attributed to men," such as aggression, power, and an emphasis on monetary gain, rather than on relationships—are more likely to face sexist behavior and other exclusionary tactics.

In such an environment, women lawyers "might be viewed as intruders and a formidable threat to men who then evoke subtle but effective strategies for protecting the boundaries of their domains" (Rosenberg, Perlstadt, and Phillips 1993:430). Sexist behavior, disparagement, discrimination, and harassment are some of the ways in which men might attempt to preserve their social place (Miller 1997; Pierce 1995; Rosenberg, Perlstadt, and Phillips 1993; Epstein 1970). Rosenberg and colleagues (1993:429) note that harassment, in particular, "is not primarily sexual behavior but, rather, a form of aggression aimed at stabilizing gender stratification." Thus, the theory of sex-typed jobs argues that women are discouraged from entering a field due to the perception that the field is a male one and, those who do enter the profession, often face exclusionary tactics and are "blocked from the opportunity structure" (Epstein 1970:967).

Whether women achieve lower levels of participation and success in the legal profession due to choice, socialization, or discrimination, it is indisputable that those who do enter the profession report gender discrimination at a number of different levels. The following section examines these claims of discrimination, exploring discrimination reported in both prior research and that discussed in the Greedy Associates community.

Gender Inequality in the Legal Practice: Prior Research and Data from an Internet Community

Studies of women in the legal profession have uncovered a variety of types of discrimination experienced by female attorneys. Discrimination can be as blatant as denying a woman a promotion based on her sex or quid pro quo sexual harassment, and as subtle as embracing participation in masculine activities and interactions as a primary means of advancement. In this section, I examine the spectrum of discrimination reported by women attorneys in both past research, and within the Greedy Associates community. As detailed in the following text, the reported experiences of many Greedy Associates' members closely parallel those of subjects in offline studies. The similarity of experiences lends credence to the notion that the experiences of Greedy Associates community members could be comparable in many ways to those of women attorneys as a whole. More importantly, however, the experiences reported in the online community assist in identifying the types of experiences for which an attorney might seek advice within a Web site environment.

Gaining Access to the Gossip Network

The barriers to success faced by women attorneys are perhaps nowhere more evident than in the act of gaining access to the gossip network. An important determinant of success in a legal career is the ability to become part of a partner network, in which an associate becomes privy to inside firm information, such as news about promotions, associate performance, gossip about the personal lives of partners or associates, and other valuable information. Gaining access to such information is both a sign of prestige for an associate, and a manner in which the associate can build bonds with partners and thereby gain work and promotions (Epstein 1970; Pierce 1995; see also Kanter 1977 for general discussion about "old boy's networks" and advancement). As a result, it becomes important for associates to learn what activities will gain them access to the gossip network, as well as to learn the manner in which to engage in those activities.

Unfortunately, research supports the notion that "women still have a hard time gaining admission to the old-boy network" and engaging in "informal socializing with male colleagues" (Pierce 1995:106–107; see also Epstein 1970). Pierce observes that "[i]n large law firms, such socializing is an important mechanism for obtaining interesting or important cases and information for garnering trust and political capital with influential partners" (1995:106–107). As a result of their exclusion from the networks, women are unable to gain access to "situations in which they can learn and are also excluded from the social control system which lets them know how well they perform" (Epstein 1970:972).

Previous research indicates that discrimination by male attorneys not only prevents women from gaining access to the network, but women who do attempt to participate in the network are discouraged in those attempts through male implementation of "boundary heightening." Boundary heightening involves emphasizing and exaggerating differences between a dominant and subordinate group (Kanter 1977). When female attorneys attempt to interact with male attorneys in the activities required to gain access to networks, male attorneys frequently engage in behavior and discuss subjects that are typically viewed as masculine. For example, male attorneys might talk about "stereotypical male topics such as sports when women are present and... [turn] social events such as after-hours drinks into competitions. Such behavior serves, consciously or not, to underscore the differences between women and men, thereby constantly reminding the women that they are different and do not fit in" (Pierce 1995:107).

Members of the Greedy Associates community frequently recount gaining access to the gossip circle as problematic, supporting the seriousness of this barrier to career advancement. When describing the importance of the gossip circle of a large New York firm, one male attorney states that "[a]ssociates rank themselves according to how much gossip they get from a partner" (*shearman suks*, 11246, 2/23/02). His comment highlights the fact that access to the gossip circle is viewed as a sign of prestige among associates. Further, he emphasizes that access to the firm's gossip circle increases the likelihood of success within the firm:

> [An associate's] work might suck and they might show up to work according to their own schedule, but if an associate can break through a partner's ego and make the partner feel slick and powerful sharing secret information with that associate...then the associate is golden. (*shearman suks*, 11246, 2/23/02)

Women within a firm, however, do not have equal access to this career enhancer:

> So how do you kiss ass and get into the partner gossip loop? Depends on whether you're male or female. Women have it the worst because they better be on the plus side of good-looking. Then they can get away with anything if they flirt with the right partners. But they still have to flirt in the right way. Lord help those that aren't good looking (as often described by partners) because then they have to play the guy games. (*shearman suks*, 11246, 2/23/02)[3]

Women working in the firm, according to some community members, must rely primarily on their physical attractiveness to gain access to the partner gossip network. Responding to a message regarding women being retained by a law firm according to their level of attractiveness, another male attorney described a similar reliance on physical attractiveness in gaining recognition within a law firm:

> [N]o matter what your parents tell you or what you hear on Sesame Street, 40 percent of your success in life will depend on the image you project of yourself (i.e., how you look), 40 percent of your success in life will depend on who you know (i.e., your "political" connections, define "political" how you will) and 20 percent will be based on what you know (i.e., what skills you have). I think in Biglaw, especially at the junior associate level, knowledge and skills are relatively equal—thus, decisions can be based on how you look and who you know—THE ONLY REALLY DISTINGUISHING CHARACTERISTICS AMONG ASSOCIATES. ...Is it arbitrary? Maybe. Is it fair. Hell, I'm no Mel Gibson and I ain't no Senator's son, so I don't think it's fair. (*lion90*, 11827, 3/19/02)

These observations suggest that one's attractiveness, coupled with one's connections, are the most important determinants of success in the legal practice. If women have difficulty gaining access to important connections with partners, they may then have to rely on their attractiveness to advance, as suggested by these individuals.

Women who are not considered attractive, however, must rely on other attributes to gain access to the partner gossip network—as indicated in the earlier quote, the "unattractive" women must play the "guy games" (*shearman suks*, 11246, 2/23/02). The "guy games" are described by the same attorney as involving playing sports, consuming alcohol, and disparaging colleagues (*shearman suks*, 11246, 2/23/02). These behaviors smack strongly of the elements of hegemonic masculinity, including subordinating other males and females to lower status, being in charge, and being physically strong (Connell 1995). Playing sports and consuming alcohol demonstrate masculine strength, whereas disparaging subordinate male and female colleagues evinces an aura of authority. It is unsurprising that attorneys who have participated in interviews or surveys, as well as members of the Greedy Associates community, have reported these same three activities as being important determinants of gaining access to desirable networks.

The Importance of Sports

Both sports playing and watching play a large role in male hegemony; in fact, "sport has come to be the leading definer of masculinity in male culture, teaching men the importance of strength, skill, and overcoming pain to compete with others" (Connell 1995; see also Kilduff and Mehra 1996). In the hypermasculine profession of law, engaging in sports participation, spectatorship, and dialogue appears to be virtually a job requirement for attorneys working at law firms. Men, in comparison to women, are more likely to both participate in sports and to be invited to participate in sporting-related activities; as a result, they gain access to important networking opportunities. Women have reported that male attorneys develop relationships with their superiors by participating in sporting activities, such as golf, but women are not similarly included in these outings (Pierce 1995).

Attorneys in the Greedy Associates community similarly report an emphasis on sports within the legal profession. One male attorney observes that "[m]ales have to play in fantasy football or baseball leagues" and "playing a sport...and golf are part of the job description in the smaller office" (*shearman suks*, 11246, 2/23/02). The opportunity to gain access to the partner gossip circle through sports participation or spectatorship is often more readily available to male attorneys than female attorneys, as indicated by one female attorney who stated that "women are going to feel out of the loop when male partners invite male associates to join their basketball leagues" (*vanilla*, 15700, 11/05/02). Members of the Greedy Associates community, therefore, not only recognize that there is a need to participate in sports to advance, but they also acknowledge that women have fewer opportunities to take advantage of this form of networking.

Advancement through Alcohol Consumption

In addition to sports participation and spectatorship, alcohol consumption is another method by which attorneys gain access to the partner gossip networks. Research indicates that those lawyers who work with other attorneys, such as in a law firm environment, are more likely to drink due to the "ready availability of colleagues with whom to drink, the presence of norms that permit or encourage work-related drinking, or the pressure to compete and rise in the firm" (Shore 2001:652; Trice and Roman 1978; Trice and Sonnenstuhl 1990; Ames and Rebhun 1993). Despite the ability to advance through the consumption of alcohol, women attorneys engage in this activity less than men. Shore (2001) found that women attorneys engaged in less frequent business-related drinking than their male counterparts, which she attributes to a lack of opportunity to conduct business over alcohol. Similarly, among attorneys who engaged in social drinking related to work, women drank less frequently and consumed fewer drinks when they did drink than men (Shore 2001).

Attorneys in the Greedy Associates community also made note of the importance of drinking to the occupation. One male attorney chronicled the amount of money an attorney must make per month to cover bills, and stated that his total did not even include "the alcohol—cause you know all us lawyer's [sic] drink a lot" (grinder, 4220, 12/16/00). Other attorneys commented on the role alcohol consumption plays in career advancement, as well as in conducting firm business. One male attorney emphasized that "[d]rinking is a plus, especially shots" if one wishes to gain access to the partner gossip network (shearman suks, 11246, 2/23/02), suggesting that the consumption of large quantities of hard alcohol might be an important part of advancement. Another attorney wondered whether firm decisions were made by "men in bars ridiculing associates," indicating that important firm decisions and firm information is exchanged by men gathering together in the joint pursuit of alcohol consumption (voice from hell, 11813, 3/19/02). Many community members evidently view drinking with partner-level attorneys as a method of gaining access to firm information and to the partner gossip network. If, as Shore (2001) found, women are less likely to consume alcohol, and consume a smaller amount when they do drink, then they will not have equal access to this avenue of advancement.

Disparaging One's Colleagues

The third method attorneys report as a means for gaining access to partner networks is through the disparagement of one's colleagues—the women in particular (Rosenberg,

Perlstadt, and Phillips 1993; Pierce 1995). Rosenberg and colleagues (1993) found that approximately two-thirds of women attorneys reported verbal disparagement related to their gender. These disparaging comments included being addressed by demeaning phrases, such as "honey" or "dear," or having remarks directed at them that emphasized their gender and/or physical appearance, such as that it is "nice to have a pretty face" (Rosenberg, Perlstadt, and Phillips 1993:422). These types of comments were more common experiences for women under 35 who worked in law firms (92 percent), as compared to those working for government agencies (65 percent) or for courts (33 percent). These findings indicate that law firm culture is perhaps particularly conducive to the disparagement of women. To this end, Rosenberg and colleagues observe that "[i]t may be that, in the private sector, a professional ethos that embodies competitive models of achievement and masculinized ideals of lawyerly behavior exists that accounts for the reports of stronger resistance to women than evidenced in public sector workplaces" (1993:423). Ultimately, Rosenberg and colleagues conclude that "regardless of whether or not they found these remarks offensive, merely annoying, or even innocuous, many of the women lawyers had to cope with frequent reminders of gender differences that are demeaning and call the legitimacy of their claims to professional equality into question" (1993:423). Similarly, Pierce (1995:108) found that through the use of disparaging remarks, "male attorneys remind women they are not part of the 'male culture'... by deflating women's occupational status."

Members of the Greedy Associates community also report a high rate of disparaging remarks in the legal profession, supporting past research that indicates law firm culture breeds this type of interaction. Disparaging remarks, although directed at all attorneys, are particularly focused on women, and participation in the activity of disparagement appears to be an important method of career advancement. One male attorney observes that men can gain access to the partnership network if they are "willing to sit behind closed doors with other guys (one partner mandatory) and disparage colleagues (especially women)" (*shearman suks*, 11246, 2/23/02). Yet another attorney described a law firm that "constantly has a bunch of 'boys' behind closed doors (with partners) talking about the non-legal attributes of women" (*ssalum*, 8018, 11/06/01).

If men do not engage in these discussions, community members report that they may face repercussions. One male attorney noted that a man either "participated in the back-door discussions of a woman's anatomy and raised his hand when the guys around the room asked 'who did her' ot [*sic*] he tried to be more dignified. If he didn't go for the bait, he was ostracized. Just ask any current male associate what the discussion is like" (*ssalum*, 8084, 11/07/01). On the other hand, one man reported that a male attorney who was previously terminated was rehired, despite poor work quality, because he "was willing to sit around with the rest of the boys club and compare the physical attributes of female co-workers" (*voice from hell*, 10541, 1/20/02). Thus, it appears that many members of the community believe that participating in the disparagement of female colleagues can perhaps "make or break" a male attorney's career.

Past research, supported by comments in the Greedy Associates community, indicates that attorneys must engage in overtly aggressive, traditionally masculine acts to gain access to the firm gossip circle, such as sports participation or spectatorship, alcohol consumption, and disparaging colleagues, particularly women colleagues. All of these activities could be designed to specifically exclude women from the partnership network by emphasizing characteristics that are typically considered to be masculine. One male attorney makes evident that he believes that these acts make it more difficult for women to assimilate into the firm culture:

> It is tough for a woman to fit in to [sic] all this and keep their sense of dignity. If you doubt that, go ask any of the women who were disproportionately [terminated]. (*shearman suks*, 11246, 2/23/02)

Good Looks: Blessing or Curse?

In the practice of law, a woman's physical appearance has also been viewed as playing a significant role in her level of success in a law firm. Physical attractiveness can result in sexual harassment, or it can result in advancement. Some studies have shown that attractive lawyers earn more money and are more likely to attain partnership status than individuals deemed less attractive (see e.g., Biddle and Hamermesh 1998). Nonetheless, attractive women who do succeed are often viewed as successful only due to their appearance. A woman's appearance, therefore, frequently becomes a focal point in her ability to climb the ladder within law firms.

The role of physical appearance in determining a woman's success is frequently raised in the Greedy Associates community. In particular, many individuals pondered whether being attractive affects both the amount of work a woman associate receives, and whether the woman is retained in the event of a firm downsizing. For women attorneys, there exists a kind of catch-22 connected with level of attractiveness. As one male attorney described it, the situation

> is a non-win for women. If she's smart, she'll get ripped apart if she's not model quality or, if she is pretty, that will dominate the discussion of her. If she isn't smart, they'll talk about how she's only around for other reasons. (*ssalum*, 8018, 11/06/01)

Many community members report that this is exactly the predicament facing women at firms. A downsizing occurred at a large firm that resulted in an uproar in the community after news came out that women were disproportionately terminated and, that of the women who remained, many were the more attractive women with weak work records (*shearmanize*, 8005, 11/06/01; *S&S Survivor*, 8087, 11/07/01). One of the most telling stories circulating on the board was as follows:

> A friend just told me there is a pretty Asian girl…who billed no more than a few hundred hours in the last year, never did any real work of any sort, spent most of her time on makeup and shopping, yet passed the layoff review with flying colors. Does anyone know what the scoop is? Any special ties? Special relationship with any of the partners? (*shearmanize*, 8005, 11/06/01)

The retention of an attractive associate, known to be a low biller, resulted in this attorney assuming that the associate had a relationship with one of the partners. Many others assumed the same about attractive female associates who were retained—that they either had an actual sexual relationship with a partner, or flirted and played the game well enough that they were retained despite the lack of such a relationship:

> Without mentioning ethnicity, there were many "gamey" women who are known to do sub-par work who were spared while women who acted more "professionally" and did good work were [not] spared. Yes, I can vouch for that first-hand. (*S&S Survivor*, 8013, 11/06/01)

The same male attorney detailed the nature of "gamey" female attorneys:

> A partner (or, more often, a Counsel) will not hide his attraction for a person and engage in flirtation, some-times over the appropriate line. Some women will just ignore it and, the best ones, gracefully deflect it. Others encourage it and it becomes very obvious that the boys will develop a "soft spot" for these women (those are the gamey ones). So if a gamey person turns in bad work, or disappears from the office to see a movie, the powers that be will dismiss it. But if someone decided that the advances weren't welcome and stayed at work rather than see a movie, they're probably on the unemployment line right now. (*S&S Survivor*, 8026, 11/06/01)

Attractive women who were willing to engage in flirta-tious behavior were more likely to be retained or to earn extra work, whereas "[w]omen who didn't play the game, or weren't pretty enough to be invited, were relegated to a lower status. Work quality didn't matter. Hours didn't matter" (*ssalum*, 8084, 11/07/01).

Community members also view female attractiveness as playing a role in the assignment of work. One individual described the manner in which flirtations that seemed like "innocent games crossed the line into determining who got good work. Then it all just blew up when the games became the driving criteria for terminations" (*shearman suks*, 11247, 2/23/02). Another attorney posted an article about a firm in which the associates drafted a memorandum describing a variety of firm ills. Among the questions asked in the memorandum was "If the assignment process isn't corrupt, ask yourself: why aren't attractive female associates ever out of work?" (*Fresh Prince*, 15479, 10/26/02). The notion that, for women, attractiveness plays an important role in acquiring work and long-term success is a pervasive one. One woman reported the difficulty posed for women who were unattractive or who did not play sexual games with partners:

> i found that i was placed in a ridiculous position because many women used the flirtation game to get ahead. they created an expectation that playing the sex game was the norm. when i rebuffed advances i was considered anti-social and ignorant as to reality. truth was that i knew exactly what i was doing but the women who flirted ended up in one of three places. used and discarded. engaged to a partner. or... using their charms to threaten a partner for favors. i ended up ok but there's much to be said about lawyers who play up the slut angle. (*uconngirl*, 20481, 7/08/04)

Some community members viewed the issue differently, however. Rather than seeing attractive females as playing a game to acquire work or keep their job, these individuals noted that attractive women attorneys are viewed as relying on their looks to succeed, even when this is not the case. One female attorney summed up the situation, saying that "[o]f course male colleagues are going to suspect that the attractive women are getting special treatment," indicating her view that attractive females are unfairly viewed as relying on their physical characteristics, rather than their intelligence, to succeed (*vanilla*, 15700, 11/05/02).

Resenting such suggestions that attractive females succeed based upon their looks, one attorney requested that members "stop all the...inferences that...any attractive females left at [the firm] only kepyt [sic] their jobs because they flirt (let [sic] just call them whores)" (*Paper Pusher*, 11853, 3/20/02). Similarly, the same attorney later indicated that people should be careful not to "imply that the only women left at [the firm] are the one [sic] that sleep with the partners" (*Paper Pusher*, 8119, 11/07/01). Even among those who accepted that attractive women did not use their appearance to advance, however, some comments indicate that attractive women are less likely to be viewed as serious about their career or to receive favorable assignments. One man stated,

> i cannot think of a single woman made partner at my old firm for whom the "slut angle" would be a remotely appropriate description. for one, most were married (to people outside the firm—not even potential business sources) and had children (or had children soon after making partner). the others, well let's just say that physical attractiveness was not part of what they brought to the table as lawyers. the good looking women mostly bailed before partnership decisions were made, usually after marrying a guy that made it possible for them to not worry about having to make money. (*eyestrain*, 20484, 7/08/04)

Another male attorney observed that female attorneys, as much as male attorneys, play a role in diminishing the abilities of attractive females:

> Don't forget that men don't make all the decisions!!! Your biggest problem, with regard to appearance, is usually going to be other women. ...They are much more prone than men are to accusing the latest young beauty in the

office of manipulating men through smiles, arm or shoulder touching, eyelash-batting and kiss-ass chatting. They closely monitor their junior co-gender members for hair-flipping, riotous laughter at male partner jokes, or other signs of wanting to be liked by men (almost always for personal advancement). Then they (the senior women) treat them (the junior cuties) like [censored] on a deal as revenge, and offer the plum assignments to the clever lad down the hall. (*thisonegoesto11*, 24616, 5/16/05)

Some community members, then, suggest that attractiveness can play a detrimental role for a female attorney.

There does not seem to be a consensus among community members as to whether attractive females are benefited by their physical appearance in any way, whether they actively seek this benefit, or whether disgruntled coworkers choose to attribute the success of attractive female attorneys to their appearance. Community member comments, however, do lend support to past research that suggests female attractiveness can affect the manner in which a woman is perceived by her coworkers and can open a woman up to being preyed upon by other attorneys, regardless of her level of attractiveness—if she is attractive, she might feel pressured to flirt to maintain her standing; if she is not attractive, she might find increased difficulty in attaining work or success in the legal field.

Femininity and the Law Firm Environment

Given the above discussion regarding the benefits and detriments of being an attractive female attorney, one might wonder whether there would be any advantage to a woman in portraying herself as more or less feminine—in both dress, and in manner. Kanter (1977) observes that women who work in a male-dominated occupation tend to select from one of four methods of self-presentation: (1) playing the mother and comforter to male coworkers, (2) acting as the seductress or sex object, (3) adopting the role of kid sister by championing the ideas of male coworkers and engaging in nonthreatening humor, or (4) acting as the "iron maiden" by demanding respect and insisting on recognition of one's competency. Regardless of the chosen coping mechanism, Kanter (1977) notes that a woman's persona is frequently misinterpreted by male coworkers. If she chooses a more feminine approach, she is often perceived as weak and has emphasized her differences from her male counterparts; if she chooses a masculine approach, she is viewed as aggressive and threatening. As a result, women in male-dominated workforces are often isolated and confused as to the best method of interaction with their coworkers and whether and how to display their femininity.

Kilduff and Mehra (1996) observe that many women who find themselves working in a very masculine workforce choose to emphasize their femininity to accommodate the interests and desires of men, including embracing feminine dress and engaging in flirtation. Emphasized femininity prevails in a dominant patriarchal culture, as it embraces an ideal that oppresses alternative types of femininity (Connell 1987). In a hypermasculine profession like that of law, women who engage in "aggression and intimidation" are viewed as having stepped outside of their gender role and could face sanctions; this threat of sanctions at times results in women choosing not to practice law in the same way as men to avoid such sanctions (Pierce 1995; see also Leahy 1994). For instance, women are more likely to present a caring ethic in the practice of law, focused on trust and respect, as opposed to an adversarial ethic, focused on suspicion and combativeness (Pierce 1995). At the same time, however, women who are not perceived as "aggressive and intimidating" are frequently viewed as incompetent in the legal practice.

It becomes apparent, therefore, that "women, unlike men, encounter a double bind between the role of the 'good woman' and the emotional requirements of the adversarial role" (Pierce 1995:104). Consequently, women are expected to both dress and act in a "feminine" manner, but those who do are viewed as not being aggressive enough to succeed in the practice of law. As described by Leahy (1994) in the context of nontraditional relationships, departures from traditional notions of femininity serve as a challenge to the very concept of emphasized femininity; as a result, these behaviors are often viewed as subversive and are frequently both rejected and discouraged.

Due to this dichotomy, it is perhaps not surprising that views of community members are mixed as to whether portraying oneself as feminine is a benefit or a hardship. One female attorney stated that if being feminine

> mean[s] cutesy flirtation, don't even think about it. They [meaning the male attorneys] hold all the cards, and it would be delusional to think otherwise. It is safe to be "feminine" around other female attorneys. When you are with the guys, try to be one of the guys. (Of course it won't work, but it's your second-best bet. Your best bet is to be adopted by a female mentor.) (vanilla, 15688, 11/05/02)

Other community members echoed the idea that female attorneys must be "one of the guys" to succeed. One woman noted that, to be successful,

> women have to be very manly. Women are generally seen as frail, passive, emotional and whiny be [sic] their male

counterparts. I've heard from several women that men made sexist comments to them and even accused them of using feminine wiles to further themselves. For instance, one female attorney at a large firm said that a male attorney accused her of wearing "flattering" clothing in order to entice associates, partners, and clients, and that he felt she was getting preferential treatment. Some people have advised me not to be to [sic] girly, whatever that means, and to be butch or bitchy! (*bruinette*, 15698, 11/05/02)

The notion that women must be "one of the guys," "manly," "butch," and avoid clothing that is too sexy indicates a belief from the community members that women cannot convey any sign of femininity if they wish to appear to be strong enough to succeed in the aggressive legal environment. The earlier discussion that women must try to play the "guy games" to gain access to the partner gossip network supports this idea of women finding success by acting like "one of the guys."

Other community members, however, argue that women will not succeed through portraying themselves as strong and "manly." Rather, one female attorney argues, a woman who seems "[t]oo into work… [is] labeled as a cold lesbian. Try to be professional, escpecially [sic] in presentation, and try to manage a situation [in a manner] that show[s] both professionalism and an ability to get along with everyone, you are a tease/slut trying to use your feminine charms to make up for performance" (*Mistress Stern*, 15745, 11/07/02). In other words, argues the woman, "[t]he law firms set up an environment that leave us struggling to appease everyone, INCLUDING OTHER WOMEN, with a constant risk of offending the wrong person."

As a result, it appears just as unclear to community members whether it is preferable to portray oneself as feminine or masculine, as whether it is more or less advantageous to be an attractive female attorney. As indicated by past research, women are perhaps encouraged by the law firm environment and the nature of legal practice to appear aggressive and therefore "manly," but at the same time men frequently view women who are more aggressive as unfeminine, cold, and "lesbian." In other words, such behavior by women is necessary for success in the legal practice due to the aggressive, adversarial nature of the practice, but women are seen as aberrant and unnatural if they engage in this behavior. It truly seems to be a "no-win" situation, very much the "double bind" described by Pierce in which women are punished whether they display the caring, relational characteristics expected of women or the adversarial characteristics necessary for success in the legal field.

Female Mentors: A Possible Solution?

The requirement of "playing the guy games," harassment based on physical appearance, and a culture that requires women to be both "feminine" and aggressive, all pose serious obstacles to advancement for women attorneys. One of the greatest challenges to success for women lawyers is that of overcoming these barriers to find a strong mentor to become an advocate. This predicament is frequently raised by members of the Greedy Associates community. One male attorney observed that male partners tend to select male associates to mentor, highlighting the fact that women attorneys are underserved in terms of mentoring:

> you'll have 10 female partners trying to mentor 100 female associates at a firm while 40 male partners mentor the 100 male associates. guess which ones are going to get more mentoring? (eyestrain, 20470, 7/08/04)

Some community members recognize this fact, and feel that female mentors are an important means by which to retain women attorneys in the field of law and assist them in their advancement. According to one attorney, "[y]our best bet is to be adopted by a female mentor" if you wish to succeed in the legal field (*vanilla*, 15688, 11/05/02). She later observed that women mentors offer some benefits to female associates:

> What they can offer to junior women attorneys is the opportunity to develop professionally without having to constantly police for sexual tension, always walking that line between not being unfriendly and not being "too friendly". Also, it is far less likely that a senior woman attorney will keep another woman at a distance in order to insulate her (meaning the junior) from crude jokes, off color language, etc. (*vanilla*, 15692, 11/05/02)

According to this community member, female mentors can allow a female associate to avoid sexual pressure, as well as the pressure to behave in a more feminine or more masculine way.

Other attorneys in the community felt that women mentors did not offer a noticeable advantage in comparison to male mentors, however. As one woman argued,

> women mentors can be part of the solution. Unfortunately, as it stands right now, many senior women attorneys have internalized institutional sexism (they had no choice other than to play the game if they were to get ahead) to such a degree that they're just as bad as the men. (*trin*, 15689, 11/05/02)

Another attorney agreed that women attorneys who have spent enough time in the law firm environment to become a mentor are also likely to have adopted the patriarchal, sexist viewpoint that dominates the field:

> Women who make it into the partnership ranks tend to suffer from Stockholm syndrome. They also tend to be relatively isolated within these institutions. (*vanilla*, 15692, 11/05/02)

This viewpoint is echoed by Kilduff and Mehra (1996), who observe that some women cope with male hegemony in the workplace by identifying with it and becoming surrogate males, internalizing the values of ruthless capitalism and domination. This practice led one female community member to note that "other women are the worst enemies to a good-looking and competent female associate" (*Mistress Stern*, 15745, 11/07/02), indicating distrust, rather than support, of a woman partner's ability to assist an associate to succeed.

Community members' mixed reports regarding the benefits of women mentors support past research indicating that women mentors cannot always advance the interests of women associates. To succeed in the law firm environment, many women have been forced to conform to the behavior and viewpoints of the males in the field and do not offer a true alternative viewpoint for female associates. In other words, senior women attorneys might have played as "one of the boys" for too long.

Conclusion

Prior research has detailed many of the challenges faced by women when attempting to enter the law firm culture. These findings suggest that the law firm environment is an adversarial one, and participants are expected to engage in behaviors that are traditionally seen as masculine. Women who seek to play the game aggressively, however, are frequently labeled as deviant. Women who do not opt to play the men's game are accused of being weak, incompetent, or are accused of playing upon their femininity to advance. In this way, women attorneys are expected to present themselves as possessing traditionally feminine traits, while the occupation demands that they exhibit traditionally masculine traits. Women mentors are viewed by some as a way to escape from this "double bind," in that perhaps women mentors would not place the same demand on women attorneys to engage in the "guy games"; however, some research indicates that female mentors are ineffective advocates for female associates.

These findings are echoed by members of the Greedy Associates community, suggesting that the concerns voiced by community members are indicative of many of the common concerns facing associates in the practice of law. Further, the Web site members' concerns depict the types of complaints of gender inequality for which attorneys might seek counsel within an online community.

As detailed in this chapter, other research has examined gender inequality in the legal practice, providing detailed accounts of perceived discrimination faced by female attorneys. There have, however, been few attempts to take the next step and assess what can be done to correct for these inequalities. The following chapters examine possible methods by which attorneys in the Greedy Associates community engage in the dispute process: coming to recognize a harm, assert blame, and—ultimately—raise a claim.

4

The Dispute Process in the Greedy Associates Community

The intricacies of party disputes have often been the subject of study by sociolegal scholars. Inquiry has focused, in particular, on the frequency of lawsuits and the outcome of those suits. Little is known, however, regarding the dispute process *before the filing of a lawsuit*. Specifically, the manner in which individuals recognize harms and choose to pursue, or not to pursue, a legal claim for remedy remains relatively unexamined (Felstiner, Abel, and Sarat 1980–1981, but see Mather and Yngvesson 1981; Sarat and Felstiner 1988). Gaining an understanding of the manner in which individuals label an experience as an actionable harm and opt to pursue a remedy can provide valuable insight into the utility of the law for addressing harms. To provide an effective plan to remedy gender discrimination, women must first recognize that an experience is, in fact, injurious, assign blame to someone other than themselves, and choose to make a demand for remedy (Felstiner, Abel, and Sarat 1980–1981). This process might seem a simple one, but for many individuals the recognition of actionable harm and the corresponding decision to pursue a remedy is a difficult, drawn-out process.

Chapters 5 and 6 examine the manner in which community members embrace, or reject, both litigation and legal discourse when challenging gender inequality. Before selecting litigation or legal discourse to challenge a harm, however, a woman must arrive at the realization that she *has been harmed* and that she wishes to seek redress in some format (be it through litigation or legal discourse). This chapter explores the manner in which the Greedy Associates community can perhaps assist attorneys in progressing through the dispute. How do female attorneys determine that gender discrimination has occurred, and that they should seek redress? In addition, how does participation in the online community assist them in reaching a decision as to whether they have been harmed and what action should be taken? Further, in what manner does the community permit attorneys to both demand a remedy, and receive a response, from their employers? In other words, how might this process within the community differ from dispute processes occurring offline? This chapter explores these issues and assesses whether interactions within the community are likely to result in encouraging or discouraging mobilization against discrimination.

The Dispute Process

Discourse plays an important role in the dispute process, given that the articulation and exchange of ideas can assist in formulating notions of wrongs and claims of entitlement. Discourse, consequently, is an invaluable resource in bringing about change; injuries and responsible parties must first be identified, and claims to rights or compensation can then be made. Felstiner, Abel, and Sarat (1980–1981) provide a framework for understanding the initial phases of the dispute process, contending that a dispute does not fully arise until the process of naming, blaming, and claiming have been completed. They assert that it is during these three phases that the most attrition occurs in individuals seeking remedy for harms: people neglect to identify a claim as an injury, they fail to blame an external party for the injury, or they opt not to pursue a grievance. These three phases are played out in the Greedy Associates community, resulting in some individuals appearing to drop their disputes, while others are aided in formulating their dispute through the interactive online process.

Naming

During the naming phase, an individual must recognize a problem as an injury (Felstiner, Abel, and Sarat 1980–1981). In other words, the problem must be recognized as a harm inflicted on the individual by an outside force before a true dispute can develop. This perhaps seems a simple step to take, as one might assume that an individual certainly knows when s/he has been harmed. Notions of what constitutes an injury, however, vary widely for many types of experiences; these varying views are often linked to race, gender, or class (Felstiner, Abel, and Sarat 1980–1981). For instance, although women might be quick to label sexual harassment as injurious, men might be more likely to view the same behavior as harmless flirtation—just "boys being boys." Felstiner and colleagues (1980–1981) argue that the naming phase is perhaps the most significant phase in the dispute process, as the type of disputes present in a society and the level to which disputes will be escalated depends heavily on what is perceived as being injurious. For example, asbestos litigation did not arise until shipyard workers began to view health problems associated with their work as an injury inflicted on them, rather than suffering necessarily intertwined with their occupation (Felstiner, Abel, and Sarat 1980–1981). Similarly, sexual harassment was not proffered a legal remedy until such practices were deemed injurious to women, as opposed to acceptable practices in a male-dominated workforce (see MacKinnon 1979 for a discussion of the development of sexual harassment law).

An individual can complete the naming phase in a number of ways. The person might perceive on his or her own that an injury has occurred; alternatively, the assistance of others might be required to arrive at the conclusion that an experience is, in fact, an injury. Within the Greedy Associates community, attorneys reach the naming phase in both of these manners. When raising gender issues, attorneys tend to enter the conversation having already labeled the experience as an injury. One attorney posting at the Greedy Associates community instigated a discussion by stating that "i got a zero bonus, and i wonder if this is because i am on maternity leave. i would appreciate any help as to how to deal with this matter. i worked very hard throughout my pregnancy (with almost nobody paying attention to my condition) and feel that i deserve at least a small piece of the pie, e.g. to ask pro-rata for the months that i worked?" (*yula*, 16384, 12/31/02). This individual evidently had already labeled her problem as an injury, as exemplified by her belief that the lack of a bonus was attributable to her maternity leave, as well as her proffered defense that she had worked hard and was deserving of such a bonus. She does not ask other board members whether she was injured; rather, she asks how she should proceed in escalating the dispute. Similarly, another woman in the community clearly has named her experience as an injury before posting on the board, stating "I am facing a sexual harassment problem and want to know if anyone out there has any advice. I've been at my firm for 2 yrs now...and i have always liked working here until the last few months where one of the jr. partners in my dept. has been making sexual advances towards me" (*bostonlawgirl*, 20465, 7/08/04). This attorney initiates her discussion by identifying her experience as an injury: sexual harassment. Although she is asking for advice, her request (as will be explored later) concerns obtaining suggestions as to how to deal with the injury, rather than assistance in labeling it as such.

When examining general working conditions, however, some individuals do not readily identify an experience as injurious, or are clearly seeking assistance in doing so. One attorney begins a post, stating, "I need advice. I am wondering if it is fairly common for firms to fire associates on a pretext of poor performance when the problem is, in fact, that the firm's business is down?" (*squeakywheel*, 18036, 5/31/03). Although the attorney has identified a problem—termination—he or she is seeking affirmation as to whether an injury has truly occurred. Through the use of the phrase "fairly common," the attorney indicates that he or she is unsure as to whether terminating an employee in this situation is acceptable. Due to this uncertainty in identifying the experience as an injury, the remainder of the attorney's message focuses on the manner in which he or she can acquire a new position. This progression indicates that the attorney's focus is more on how the termination will affect job prospects, rather than on whether an injury has occurred. Board members, in turn, responded by offering suggestions as to how to interview for a new position following this type of termination,

but some also identified the problem as injurious and eval-
uated the chances for a successful lawsuit (one going so far
as to encourage a suit) (*zennist1*, 18436, 7/12/03).
Exploration of the problem is often necessary to label it
an injury but, at times, individuals need encouragement
to explore a problem (Jefferson 1988). Thus, trouble narra-
tives can be coproduced, as the listener can ask questions
or express sympathy to encourage elaboration, or can offer
stories of similar problems to aid the original speaker in
exploring the situation (Jefferson 1988). Such an instance
occurred in the case of the terminated attorney. After
hearing tales from other board members who experienced
similar problems, the attorney stated, "It is incredibly
reassuring to me to know that this has happened to others, as well" (*squeakywheel*, 18047, 6/1/03). The attorney
then proceeded to provide additional details regarding
the termination so that others might evaluate the merits
of the problem as a potential dispute. Through the provision of the additional details, the attorney sought assistance in determining whether he or she had, in fact, been
harmed. As a result, the attorney was aided by community
members in progressing from a focus on obtaining a new
position, to a situation in which he or she was developing
a claim for an injury.

In this manner, the Web community provides a unique
method for assisting attorneys in naming a problem as
injurious. The casual interaction with those who might
have experienced similar harms allows for the recognition
of injuries, given that the ability to communicate with
others can result in the discovery that some problems are
common. Because the community provides for a greater
exposure to individuals with similar lifestyles (i.e., attorneys), the likelihood of interacting with someone with a

similar experience is increased over offline interactions. Further, the anonymity of the community allows for a comfort in communicating private concerns and receiving feedback, whereas some attorneys might be hesitant to share employment issues with coworkers or friends offline. As a result, interactions in the community might aid an individual in reaching the conclusion that there is a cause for the problem, that is, that s/he has been injured, rather than the unfortunate beneficiary of an isolated, blameless harm.

In this manner, the online community can assist attorneys in reaching the first step toward identifying a dispute between law firms and associate attorneys, in situations where associates might be less clear that a harm has occurred. As indicated in the earlier examples, however, women introducing topics on gender discrimination are more likely to have already reached the naming stage without the aid of community members. As a result, for gender inequality claims, the next stage in the dispute process—blaming—becomes a more fertile ground for seeking assistance within the Web site community.

Blaming

After an experience has been identified as an injury, the person must then form a link between the injury and the party believed to have caused the injury. The injury is transformed into a grievance when fault is assigned during the "blaming process." This differs from a wish, or a complaint lodged against no one in particular, as there is a party to whom fault has been assigned and there is the hope of a remedy (Felstiner, Abel, and Sarat 1980–1981). Felstiner and colleagues (1980–1981) note that the causes a person identifies for an injury serve as significant predictors of the type of recourse that will be undertaken. If an individual fails to identify a person or entity as the party responsible for an experience and, instead, blames him or herself, it is less probable that they will view the experience as an injury or pursue a remedy.

Just as in the naming process, an individual can complete the blaming phase either on their own, or with assistance from others. In the case of the woman experiencing sexual harassment from another attorney, the party at fault was quickly identified. She explained that a junior partner engaged in the harassing behavior, and then elaborated on the situation, emphasizing his blame for the predicament:

> He only does it when no one else is around to witness it of course, and I have never done anything to encourage it (we've never seen each other socially, never seen each other even outside of work period! Etc...) and I always try to make it noticeable that I am not comfortable with any type of romantic relationship, plus he even knows I am engaged. I try and avoid being alone with him, but sometimes it's unavoidable b/c we need to meet in his office to discuss work, or travel for a client etc. (*bostonlawgirl*, 20465, 7/08/04)

Through the recitation of her experiences, she makes evident that the partner, rather than she, is at fault; she notes that she has never engaged in activities designed to encourage his overtures, she has not associated with him outside of work, and she has attempted to make her lack of interest clear. By telling her story in this manner, she indicates to other community members that she has completed the blaming phase and is seeking advice as to how to proceed in terms of addressing the situation.

Pomerantz (1978) indicates that harms are typically mentioned to others in fairly general terms, at which time the listener asks questions to determine the party responsible for the harm. At times, the individual describing the harm is unclear as to who is to blame for the injury. For instance, in the previously mentioned scenario involving the terminated attorney, the attorney began by simply noting the termination and asking for help in seeking a new position (*squeakywheel*, 18036, 5/31/03). Community members immediately began asking for details to determine whether the firm or the terminated attorney was at fault; one individual requested "without revealing too much, please provide us with more information on the circumstances surrounding dismissal. when how why" (*Yale JD*, 18039, 5/31/03).

After hearing details of the termination, some concluded that the firm was at fault, criticizing the action by stating that "many firms are firing people and saying it's for cause to keep up the impression that business is good" (e.g., *fmapirate*, 18037, 5/31/02), and some encouraged legal action against the firm (e.g., *zennist1*, 18436, 7/12/03). In contrast, other respondents suggested that the terminated attorney must be at fault, noting, for instance, that "every firing I've been a part of has been for cause—I have never seen an economic layoff" and contending that if there are economic problems, "the least productive/capable lawyers are let go first" (*1partner*, 18052, 6/1/03). In this scenario, community members talk through the situation, probing for additional information, to ascertain fault. By doing so, they perhaps aid the complainant in arriving at a decision concerning the culpability in this dispute.

In contrast, at times individuals arrive at the community, having already rendered a determination as to blame.

The determination of the complainant is not, however, accepted at face value. Instead, community members often attempt to aid in the "blaming process," even when their assistance is not requested. For instance, in the case of the woman being harassed by the junior partner, she clearly articulated the party to blame. Her version of the events, however, was rejected by many of the community members. For instance, one male attorney responded, "maybe what you view as sexual advances he views as innocent flirting? the guy isn't grabbing your ass is he? does he ask you out to romantic dinners?" (*eyestrain*, 20466, 7/08/04). There are two messages communicated by this response. First, he seems to suggest that perhaps the woman has not suffered an injury in the first place; she has misnamed "innocent flirting" as an injury. Second, he indicates that perhaps the woman attorney is too quick to blame the partner for the situation; he is not necessarily doing anything wrong, rather it is she that is responsible for overreacting to "innocent flirting." Similarly, another attorney responded:

> I have always thought that sometimes folks unduly complain about harassment. For example, I do think it is unfair, except in extraordinary situations, for someone to be accused of harassment for saying one thing or flirting if no one has directly told that person that what they are saying is offensive. If, however, they are told and then they persist, at that point I believe action should be taken. (*wormhole*, 20478, 7/08/04)

The individual thereby indicates that perhaps the blame has been misplaced. It is "unfair" to "accuse" someone of harassment, if she has not directly instructed him to refrain from the offensive actions. In this manner, this attorney seems to suggest that the "accuser" might be at fault for not fulfilling some imagined obligation to voice a clear objection to the behavior. In fact, 7 out of the 21 responses received by this particular woman raised the issue that perhaps she had failed to make her objections evident, that is, that perhaps the situation was her fault. Another nine individuals appeared to accept that the male partner was to blame in their responses, whereas the remaining responses did not address the issue of blame.

None of these interactions seemed to shake the original assessment of the woman attorney as to the correct individual *to blame*; she remained firm in her conviction that the junior partner was at fault. In response to the numerous assertions that perhaps she had misinterpreted, or failed to make her position clear, she noted, "the behavior from this jr. partner is so offensive and has become so overt physically that I can't even stay late working knowing he's still in the office down the hall from me. ... so yes... it's more than 'innocent flirting'" (*bostonlawgirl*, 20490, 7/09/04).

The interactive nature of the Web site community, therefore, can assist some individuals in advancing in the dispute process. After an injury has been identified, the ability to interact with a number of persons who are familiar with the law firm community can aid in determining the individual(s) or entity who bear the blame for the harm. At the same time, some individuals arrive in the community, having already completed the blaming phase. Discussing the situation within the community perhaps assists in challenging, or in solidifying, their assessment of the situation. Many, however, reject assistance in the blaming phase and, instead, seek guidance in moving through the claiming stage.

Claiming

The third stage of the dispute process, the claiming phase, involves asserting a right that has been violated by the alleged responsible party and requesting a remedy (Felstiner, Abel, and Sarat 1980–1981). The accused party, in turn, can offer to repair the wrong or can deny responsibility; if there is no response by the accused party, or the claim is rejected, the claim is transformed into a dispute. The Greedy Associates community serves two important functions in the claiming stage. First, members of the community are able to obtain advice as to the best manner to resolve a work dispute. They might debate the merits of confronting the offender and demanding a remedy, including monetary compensation, the cessation of an offensive action, or a promotion or accommodation. If they choose to confront the responsible party, they might opt to do so informally, face-to-face, or through formal legal venues. They might also opt not to pursue a claim at all. Community members frequently talk through the merits of pursuing a variety of these recourses. In addition to sorting through means of addressing a claim, the community also serves an important function by permitting members to lodge complaints directly against their employers in an anonymous forum; in turn, partners are able to respond to these claims within the Web site community.

Arriving at the Decision to Make a Claim
Before making a claim, individuals are likely to sort through a variety of means by which to address the grievance. In doing so, it is often helpful to engage in discussion with an audience to arrive at a decision as to how to pursue a claim. Felstiner and colleagues (1980–1981) note that the type of

response received from others concerning a grievance can impact whether an individual chooses to set forth a claim for remedy. If the reference group offers sufficient support of the claim for injury, political mobilization might ensue. Group members might also define an injury as harmless and discourage pursuit of a claim. The reaction of the group depends in part on group "subculture" (Felstiner, Abel, and Sarat 1980–1981). Lawyers, in particular, often offer the most influential responses, directing the manner in which a claim is formed or whether it is rejected. For instance, in examining the manner in which language employed in lawyers' offices affects claim formation, Sarat and Felstiner (1988) find that lawyers' responses to clients' claims tend to mold the substance of the claims. Lawyers employ legal language and reasoning to discern the significant points of an individual's claims. If an individual voices complaints that are irrelevant to a legal claim, those complaints are ignored.

Mertz (1992:426) notes that this practice results in "validating only some stories, hearing only some voices." This selective validation is significant when examining claims made by women or other disadvantaged groups. Complaints articulated by disadvantaged groups might be turned back on those who voiced the injury—for example, poverty might be attributed to the "pathology" of single mothers (Mertz 1992). If individuals receive this type of a blame-shifting response to the articulation of a grievance, they might be more inclined to drop the grievance than to pursue it. Indeed, the discussion of potential claims in the Greedy Associates community results in a variety of responses by members of the community—including legal analyses of the strengths of a claim, as well as the shifting of blame.

Returning to the example of the woman attorney alleging sexual harassment, one can see this process play out. After the woman described the situation she was facing, she sought guidance concerning means to handle the situation, stating

> I feel as if I say something i'll be killing my whole legal career-especially at this firm where there are few women partners, and even fewer female associates, and he is a jr partner whose been with the firm for 7 yrs who is really well liked by everyone (espcially the older partners). Is my only option to just leave the firm? Has anyone out there been through something similar, or seen it handled at their firm? Thanks for any thoughts! (*bostonlawgirl*, 20465, 7/08/04)

Community members were quick to respond with an assortment of advice. Six individuals suggested that she retaliate directly against the junior partner, in a variety of manners, as voiced by one individual:

> No one will agree with this advise [*sic*], but if I were you, the next time the two of you are alone and he makes an inappropriate advance or comment, I would close the door and tell him if he continues to do this you are going to first punch him in the ba!!s, then tell his wife, then your fiance who will probably beat the crap out of him. I suspect this will make him respect you more, or continue to make you miserable, which you already are. (*BaggedIt*, 20524, 7/13/04)

Rather than reporting the offender, or seeking legal action, this individual advises both physical and emotional assault to resolve the situation. Marshall (2005) found that women occasionally reported resorting to physical assault as a last resort when confronting a harasser. Notably, one rather ironic method suggested to increase the junior partner's "respect" for the harassed attorney involves engaging her fiancé to take physical action to "protect" her from the harassment of the partner. This advice is echoed by four other individuals responding to her post, which seems to suggest a strong belief that a woman might need male assistance in defending herself against harassment. These types of responses appear to be less influenced by the legal "subculture" of the community; individuals offer nonlegal retaliation as a means of recourse. At the same time, however, it is possible that these responses are influenced by an intimate knowledge of both the legal system and gender inequality in the legal practice—this knowledge could result in many viewing more formal methods of recourse as unrealistic or hazardous to one's career, as will be explored in chapter 5.

Others, however, do engage in analysis of the legal merits of a sexual harassment claim and encourage the woman to take steps toward legal action by keeping a log of offensive acts and reporting the partner to her employer. As summarized by one attorney, "Managing partners lose sleep over these kinds of things, and sexual harassment suits are often founded on far less than this. Assemble your proof, ask nicely for it to stop, and give them an opportunity to fix it. They can't fault you for that. Above all, be strong, and tough" (*wickedgreedy*, 20515, 7/12/04). Six of the 21 responses encouraged the woman to take some form of evidence gathering/reporting that would serve as the precursor for a lawsuit.

Finally, many of the responses encouraged the woman attorney to avoid addressing the problem through litigation or through the grievance process to protect her position of employment. One male attorney noted, "your career at that firm will be over if you make a complaint based on what you've described so far. and when rumors circulate (and they always do) you may be branded as a trouble-maker other places you go" (*eyestrain*, 20466, 7/08/04). Another cautioned: "I honestly think that turning this guy in will make your life at the firm miserable, so what you need to do is to stand up and demand the respect you know you deserve" (*cacciatore*, 20496, 7/09/04). Evidently, "standing up" to this individual involves actions other than reporting him to the employer. One male attorney described additional possible repercussions he associates with reporting an individual for sexual harassment:

> basically we're told never to speak to or look at anyone of the opposite sex, even the same sex if you can avoid it just in case. and then female attorneys wonder why no male partners try to be their mentors. if you're a male partner you are absolutely nuts to try and be a mentor for a young female attorney brought up in this culture of sexual harassment everywhere you look (and to construe everything as sexual harassment). way way too big a risk. (*eyestrain*, 20470, 7/08/04)

Essentially, he argues that when female attorneys report sexual harassment, they only harm themselves, as they are less likely to reap the benefits of mentoring if they are viewed as potential "troublemakers." Further, he implies that the act of reporting increases problems for women attorneys as a whole, as men will not want to mentor a woman, regardless of whether she personally has lodged a complaint. Through this message, he engages in the type of "blame-shifting" described by Mertz (1992), labeling the career harms suf-fered due to sexual harassment as the fault of the harassed, rather than the harasser. He is quickly called on this claim by another individual, who retorts: "Great. So basically it's women's fault that men won't mentor them. Why should women have to pay the price for what guys did in the good ol' days?" (*boxer*, 20472, 7/08/04).

Regardless of any attacks on the wisdom or merits of these suggestions, however, the idea was firmly put forth by many community members that reporting sexual harassment, or simply complaining to a harasser, can be harmful to a woman's career. This type of discourse might discourage a woman from making a formal complaint. Indeed, the woman attorney who originated the discussion thanked everyone for their advice and concluded "I think the only way not to ruin any chance of working for a firm ever [much less one in conservative Boston] is *to just leave*" (*bostonlawgirl*, 20490, 7/09/04; emphasis added). Through the exchange of information with other community members, she appears to ultimately arrive at the conclusion that she has no real recourse and that the only alternative is to sweep her grievance quietly under the rug and move on. Whereas the interaction with community members did not shake her conviction that she was harmed, and that the partner was to blame, the online interactions perhaps had more of an impact on her decision of whether to make a claim. Whether she ultimately pursued a claim offline is unknowable; however, the online interactions appear to have at least shifted her discourse away from litigation and toward nonlegal remedies. Marshall (2005) similarly found that seeking advice and support from coworkers, while beneficial, can also result in convincing a woman to dismiss a claim. This dismissal is a result of the woman being deterred due to her coworkers' reminders of the consequences, as well as the lack of efficacy, of pursuing a claim (Marshall 2005).

Table 4.1   Responses to sexual harassment claims by gender

Response	Men (%)	Women (%)	Undetermined (%)
Litigation	27	11	8
Report	0	0	25
Confront	10	22	34
Ignore/Leave	0	34	8
Misinterpreting	18	0	0
Male to Protect	18	22	8

The types of responses offered to this particular woman, and to other women making sexual harassment claims, do appear to vary based on the sex of the author. Table 4.1 depicts the results of a review of approximately 40 responses to descriptions of sexual harassment; percentages reflect the percent of men, for example, who responded by encouraging a particular form of action, out of all male respondents. One can see that 27 percent of the responses offered by those identified as men involved suggesting that a woman take steps toward a formal lawsuit; in contrast, approximately 11 percent of individuals identified as women suggested litigation. This finding is supported by other research that suggests that those who are less powerful, or victimized, are also likely to be distrustful of the law and hesitant to invoke its usage in their defense (Marshall 2005; Nielsen 2000; Ewick and Silbey 1998). Marshall (2005) observes that most tactics employed by women to cope with sexual harassment involve avoiding the harasser and obtaining emotional support from others. She notes that when women fear retaliation or negative repercussions that might be derived by invoking the law, then legal remedies could prove insufficient in addressing the problem (Marshall 2005).

Among the nonlegal remedies proffered, approximately 22 percent of the responses offered by women suggested confronting the offender in some manner—either by emphasizing boundaries verbally or physically, or even by reporting the behavior to the man's wife. Only 10 percent of the men who responded suggested this type of confrontation as a possible means to redress the situation. The most popular response offered by women, however, was to simply ignore and accept the behavior and/or to leave the firm; 34 percent of women offered this response compared to 0 percent of men. Sexual harassment research supports the notion that women tend to deal with sexual harassment by "ignoring it" (Marshall 2005; Quinn 2000; Nielsen 2000; MacKinnon 1979). Interestingly, one can see as well that women (22 percent) appear just as likely to suggest the use of a man for protection (boyfriend, fiancé, husband, etc.) as are men (18 percent).

The manner in which responses vary by gender demonstrates that different women might receive very different feedback on whether and how to make a claim, depending on the gender of those responding to their message. In general, approximately an equal number of men and women seem to participate in the community (see discussion in chapter 2) and, as a result, women generally receive feedback from both genders. There are moments, however, when a woman receives many suggestions of litigation as a viable recourse; these are perhaps the times when men are the primary participants on the board. Once individuals identified as women join in the discussion, however, litigation is usually critiqued and discouraged, and talk of "accepting" the problem becomes more frequent.

Interaction with Partners during the Claiming Process
In addition to permitting an exploration of means of pursuing (or not pursuing) a grievance, the community also

serves the additional purpose of permitting direct claims to employers, and hosting employers' responses to these claims. Lee (2001:874) suggests that in the face of hate speech, "placing the perpetrator and victim in a hypothetically solidaristic, communicative relationship (as members of a common speech community) rather than in an adversarial juridical relationship (as legal persons)" provides a stronger possibility for change. This would be the case especially when the dominant group suffers sanctions through public exposure from failing to engage in a dialogue with the oppressed (Lee 2001). The Greedy Associates community provides a forum for attorneys to assert rights against their employers, and permits employers the opportunity to respond, thereby initiating an open dialogue. Although this dialogue is still adversarial in nature, it is removed from the formal legal process and law firms face potential sanctions from the public by failing to respond to associate claims. As a result, law firms must take the potential for public exposure into account in deciding whether and how to respond to associates' claims of rights violations.

In one such instance, many associates raised concerns regarding fair treatment in connection with extensive layoffs at a large New York firm, contending that attractive females were saved from the layoffs, that individuals who were due retention bonuses were targeted for layoffs, that the firm misrepresented the security of associates' jobs before the layoffs to avoid associate flight, and that terminated associates were encouraged to leave early to limit their access to sensitive information that could be published on the Web community (see e.g., 599, 9138, 12/02/01; S&S Survivor, 9154, 12/03/01). After associates alleged that the firm had engaged in gender discrimination, violated wage contracts, and made misrepresentations, individuals who community members believed to be firm partners posted vehement denials of these accusations. One apparent partner labeled the associates' claims as "lies" and contended that "the longer [the firm] is the focus of these unsubstantiated attacks the harder it is for those with resumes on the street" (*HHW*, 9141, 12/02/01; *HHW*, 9168, 12/03/01). Through this response, the partner denies the claim by labeling the accusations as "lies" and attempts to encourage associates to refrain from voicing such complaints by casting them as harmful to career advancement. In response to this message, one associate countered: "It's amazing, none of you have the guts to stand up and say 'we screwed up' but you will get on here and think you can discredit associates for telling true stories" (*S&S Survivor*, 9154, 12/03/01). The associate was able to reassert the associates' accusations against the alleged partner and renew the dispute, thereby requesting future responses to the claims.

Similarly, a number of attorneys critiqued the manner in which layoffs were handled at a particular firm, suggesting that sexual favors or gender discrimination were involved in making the layoff determinations. In response, one man identified as a partner rejected these assertions, asking "Do you really believe that the partners let people go for reasons other than the bottom line?" (*Zoltar*, 11814, 03/19/02). One male attorney argued that the partner's explanations of the termination decisions "fool no one. It's what the partnership would like people to believe, but it's not going to work" (*shearmanscrewed*, 11817, 3/19/02). Through this exchange, the associates expressed their grievance, an individual identified as a partner responded and attempted to diffuse the accusations, and one of the associates reasserted the claim of discriminatory treatment—suggesting that the firm's explanations were insufficient to explain the layoff patterns. Months later, an attorney directed a message to the same partner, stating "I think it's time to answer a question you posted on the board several months ago..." (*heletrue*, 15169, 10/11/02). The associate then provides particular information concerning the billable hours of favored female attorneys in the layoffs, in comparison with other attorneys who were terminated; he challenges: "Please verify these numbers and let me know your thoughts" (*heletrue*, 15169, 10/11/02). The community, therefore, permits not only claims to be directed against the firm in general, but against particular partners—perhaps compelling a greater need for a response.

In the above-described instances, the attorneys received responses from individuals identified as partners to their claims of mistreatment. In other cases, however, there is little or no response from firms to claims voiced on the Web site. If law firms fail to respond to attorney complaints or persist in avoiding blame, associates may decide to "lump it" (Miller and Sarat 1980–1981). "Lumping it" involves giving up on the dispute and resolving to live with the injury. Claimants might choose to lump it if the dispute process appears foreboding in the initial stages, or if they are discouraged by law firms' repeated attempts to avoid blame (Miller and Sarat 1980–1981).

At least one large law firm has taken a public position of nonresponse to rights claims on the Greedy Associates site. One magazine, reporting on layoffs at a large firm, noted that associates were challenging the firm's actions at the Greedy Associates Web site; asked for their reaction, partners of the firm characterized "the anonymous message posters as 'a few angry people making a whole lot of noise.' Firm spokesman...adds that, 'It's hard to separate fact from fiction on these chat rooms, and we'd rather not comment on anonymous assertions'" (*xshearman*, 12034, 3/28/02). If firms as a whole pay no heed to associates' claims at the Web site, associates might abandon their claims, as well as the forum, as a method to voice disputes.

There are some indications, however, that associates' claims are, at the very least, being noticed by law firm partners and are eliciting some response. In response to a partner's repeated messages that associate claims were false, one associate noted:

> Don't you realize that every time one of you partners get on here, assumes a false identity and defends the firm through what turns out to be lies you just multiply the sliminess of the whole firm and reinforce how poorly managed the place really is? (*S&S Survivor*, 9154, 12/03/01)

This post indicates that partners are believed to be noticing and responding to associate claims at the Web site, although they respond primarily by denying blame for the associates' injuries. Nonetheless, the simple fact that alleged partners are posting denials of blame perhaps serves as some evidence that associates' online complaints are effective—as this associate notes, responses "reinforce" the problems apparent in the firm. The same associate later observes the attempts by partners to dilute the harm caused by accusations at the Web site:

> Self-pity may be real, but it is interesting how many [of the firm's] partners it brought to this board under disguise. [He]'s another one. We all know that....[He] doesn't

realize that we backed off after nobody at [the firm], here or elsewhere, stepped up and showed where any single fact we posted here was false. This guy just seems paranoid as though he's justifying what [the firm] did. The last time he tried to show just one misleading statement we showed that he was incorrect and he never responded. Just like [names others believed to be partners] these users mysteriously pop up to discredit anyone with a negative thing to say about the pathetic firm and then disappear. (*S&S Survivor*, 9752, 12/13/01)

The fact that individuals identified as partners feel the need to do "damage control" at the Web site seems to indicate that there is some power in the dialogue being engaged in at the site.

Conclusion

Progression through the dispute process is a necessary component of addressing perceived inequality. Attorneys facing gender inequality can, and certainly do, reach various stages of the dispute process outside of the Web site community. Nonetheless, the Greedy Associates community provides a unique forum for attorneys to engage in the dispute process, arrive at a decision concerning the means by which to pursue their claims, and voice accusations and claims against their employers. Further, the community allows law firms to respond to these claims, resulting in the ability to fully engage in all stages of the dispute process.

In many sectors of the labor force, individuals might feel more comfortable pursuing legal action against their employers or in openly accusing current and former employers of wrongs. Unions can provide some protection for employees, and employees in nonlegal areas of employment are likely less fearful that legal action will hinder their ability to secure future employment. Anonymity is important, however, in the legal field, due in part to normal concerns regarding raising disputes against an employer in the absence of union protection. In addition, though, lawyers run an even greater risk that potential future employers will learn of legal action since those employers operate within the judicial process itself. As a result, the ability to proceed through the dispute process in an anonymous forum renders the Greedy Associates community an attractive and unusual tool for pursuing complaints against employers.

In the following two chapters, the manner in which the community can assist members in arriving at the claiming stage of the dispute process is more closely examined. Specifically, chapter 5 explores community members' concerns regarding the efficacy of litigation. The way in which community members view litigation sheds light on some of the benefits and motivations of exploring disputes within the Web site forum. Chapter 6 examines an alternative method of voicing a claim: via the use of legal discourse. As articulated in chapter 6, the Web site community appears to offer particular advantages for examining claims through the assertion of legal rights.

5

Employing Litigation to Redress Gender Inequality

Many people assume that women will deal with gender inequality via litigation, particularly when that woman is a lawyer. Legal action, founded upon Title VII and state antidiscrimination laws, does provide one option for redressing sex discrimination in the workplace. This seemingly clear-cut approach, however, is oftentimes less of a panacea than it first appears. The challenges inherent in pursuing litigation are explored in this chapter, including the role of legal mobilization in lawyers' lives and the manner in which the legal system serves to discourage the use of formal litigation measures. Drawing on both sociological literature and case law, I examine some of the legal obstacles facing female attorneys in the judicial system. Building on this foundation, I then examine the discourse contained in the Greedy Associates community surrounding the use of litigation as a means for confronting gender inequality. Results indicate that attorneys in this community discourage the use of litigation to challenge gender discrimination. This reluctance appears to result from their familiarity with the daunting task of establishing a discrimination case in the judicial system, as well as the fear of inflicting damage on their careers by suing an employer. Communication of these concerns to other community members can generate, or reinforce, perceptions regarding the futility of litigation, thereby discouraging the realization of rights claims.

The Challenges Posed by Litigation

The utility of litigation in redressing harms has been disputed among legal scholars. McCann (1994) observed that legal action can result in direct effects, such as winning short-term remedial relief for victims of injustice or developing case law precedent that might affect future judicial outcomes. The notion that formal litigation can be used to create a significant alteration in the working conditions of women attorneys is, however, questionable.

The belief that litigation can be used to enact change is, according to Scheingold (1974), a "myth of rights." The myth of rights suggests that litigation results in a declaration of rights by the courts; the courts can then be used as a resource to assure the realization of these rights; and, finally, the realization of these rights is equivalent to meaningful change (Scheingold 1974). Scheingold contends that the myth of rights is problematic for a variety of reasons. Judges cannot be counted on to determine a "right" for all worthwhile social goals and, even when a right exists, an adequate remedy might not be awarded. In addition, Scheingold argues that litigation is problematic as a mode of social change because it leads to disputes between individual parties at a given point in time, rather than a more overarching political conflict that has the power to effect change. McCann (1994:5) agrees that "litigation provides at best a momentary illusion of change rather than real substantive empowerment for traditionally marginalized citizens," noting that federal courts lack the will or the capacity to correct for discrimination.

In addition, for women attempting to challenge gender inequality, it could be argued that turning to the legal system—a system in which the laws have been written, argued, and interpreted largely by men—legitimates the dominant male perspective of equality, rather than instigates change (MacKinnon 1979; Baer 1999; Schneider 1990). For instance, in examining sexual harassment law, MacKinnon (1979) argues that the law itself, as well as judicial interpretations of the law, should integrate women's experiences with sexual harassment to provide a just remedy. Women's experiences have not been incorporated into the interpretation of sexual harassment law, however, resulting in legal precedent that is notably at odds with the everyday understandings of most individuals regarding sexual harassment law. For example, in one Fifth Circuit Court of Appeals case, the court determined that a plaintiff who alleged that a coworker commented on the color of her nipples, attempted to look up and down her dress, invited her multiple times to sit in his lap, and stroked her arm and shoulders on a number of occasions, had not established a claim for sexual harassment *as a matter of law* (Shepherd v. *The Comptroller of Public Accounts of the State of Texas* 1999). The court argued that such conduct, while unseemly, was not sufficient to constitute sexual harassment, since a "reasonable" person's work would not be disrupted by the coworker's actions.

This case is not an anomaly among sexual harassment cases; rather, the burden of proof is extreme for a plaintiff to establish that sexual harassment has occurred. For instance, the *Shepherd* court noted that the type of touching that has been found to be sufficiently severe to create a hostile environment consists of instances such as when "male coworkers cornered women and rubbed their thighs, grabbed their breasts, and held a woman so that a man could touch her" (*Shepherd v. Comptroller* 1999:875, citing *Hall v. Gus Coast Co.* 1988). That the courts seem frequently to equate sexual harassment with behavior that either borders on, or is equivalent to, criminal behavior, suggests a disconnect between women's experiences with sexual harassment and the formal interpretation of the law. Such findings are likely colored by the fact that those arguing the cases and rendering the decisions are predominantly male and are less likely to have experienced sexual harassment than females. As a result, their determination as to what constitutes behavior sufficient to disrupt the working environment of a "reasonable" individual is likely colored by their gender. When women then turn to litigation to seek a remedy for sexual harassment, or other forms of gender discrimination, they are confronted by a system steeped in male domination, and perhaps ill-equipped to address their complaints.

Undoubtedly due in part to these concerns, Quinn (2000) observes that women rarely use the law to challenge sexual harassment. Rather, they are more likely to ignore sexual harassment which often results, ultimately, in quitting a position to avoid the offending behavior. Many scholars, therefore, contend that the notion that litigation can effect change is simply a myth, since the judicial process might fail to create or enforce rights and, when it does, the process is so isolated between specific disputants that social change does not result.

Further, there are particular obstacles faced by *attorneys* in selecting formal litigation as a means to challenge gender inequality. As indicated in the close of chapter 4, lawyers risk damaging their careers by engaging in formal litigation. Research indicates that women are typically in a worse position if they engage in direct confrontation of harassment, than if they choose more passive measures (Fitzgerald and Swan 1995). Lawyers, in particular, run the risk of not only harming their relationship with their current employer, but that with future employers since those employers operate within the judicial system and are likely to learn of lawsuits.

Women Lawyers Who Sued

For all of the reasons chronicled in this chapter, it would seem unlikely that women attorneys would resort to litigation in redressing claims. From my own experience in the legal practice, I knew many women who felt that they were the victims of sex discrimination or harassment; none of these women sued their employer, typically voicing concerns over the impact such an action would have on their careers. Some women, however, do file lawsuits against their employers, with varying levels of success. From a review of the published opinions in these cases, it is impossible to glean whether these women incurred career costs due to their lawsuits. An analysis of the decisions, however, provides insight into the level of success achieved by women attorneys, as well as the language used by the courts in rendering their decisions. It quickly becomes apparent that few women attorneys have filed lawsuits on which decisions are rendered, that those decisions are usually not in their favor, and that the reasoning of the decision maker is, at times, problematic.

After performing a basic case law search in Lexis-Nexis, a legal database, I located only 15 cases in which a woman attorney sued for sex discrimination or sexual harassment. These cases were those in which a judicial decision was entered, either in the summary judgment[1] phase or after a trial to the court or to a jury; consequently, cases that settled before a decision being rendered are not captured by this search.[2] Table 5.1 reveals that in 10 of the 15 cases, the plaintiff lost to the employer. In two of the six cases where law firms were the employer, the plaintiff won in a trial to the jury. In three of the five cases where the government was the employer, the government's motion for summary judgment was denied; in other words, there were enough facts in dispute for the case to proceed to trial and the facts, if found in the plaintiff's favor, were sufficient to warrant a finding of discrimination. The plaintiff lost all of the cases where the employer was a corporation. In only 13 percent of the cases, therefore, was there a clear victory for the plaintiff; in one-third of the cases, the case remained viable for the plaintiff (two wins to a trial by jury, and three cases where the defendant's motion for summary judgment was defeated). Overall, this grouping of cases seems to suggest that when women attorneys do choose to sue their employers, their odds of winning are relatively low.

A closer examination of one of these decisions sheds light on both the types of complaints made by women

Table 5.1 Summary of discrimination cases

Employer	Losses	Wins
Law Firm	4	2
Corporation	4	0
Government	2	3 (Defeated MSJ; Proceed to Trial)
Total	10	2; 3 MSJ Defeated

attorneys, as well as the language employed by the courts in rendering their analyses and decisions. In *Fitzgerald v. Ford, Marrin, Esposito, Witmeyer and Gleser*, an attorney sued a law firm under Title VII, alleging sexual harassment (*Fitzgerald v. Ford* 2001). Fitzgerald claimed that actions by other associate attorneys and by the firm's partners created a hostile work environment. She alleged that male associates engaged in open conversations about sex, including detailing their sex lives, telling jokes about women and about sex, and discussing the sex lives of partners (such as rumored homosexual activities with associates).

In addition to these general conversations, Fitzgerald complained of a number of comments specifically directed against her. For instance, both partners and associates referred to her as a "dyke," or called her "butch." Numerous comments were made regarding her attire; one attorney noted that her choice of dressing in a pants suit, rather than a skirt, was unprofessional and "butch," another encouraged her to "wear something black and lacey" to an upcoming event, and still another informed her that a sweater she was wearing was not "slutty enough." Although coworkers evidently thought she did not present herself in an ultrafeminine manner, she was nonetheless critiqued at a performance evaluation for not being aggressive enough. One partner suggested that she act more like one of the male associates, noting that if he went to a bar to pick up a woman and was turned down, he would move on to the next woman; the analogy suggested that she should be similarly aggressive. In addition, some comments directed at Fitzgerald seemed particularly suggestive of sexual favors; one attorney asked her if she wanted to "lick his fingers" after he had finished a greasy lunch and also sent her an e-mail concerning a male friend that stated "If Nantucket boy isn't getting it done, I can take care of you."

The court found that these factors did not create a hostile working environment, as a matter of law. Perhaps what is most telling about the opinion is the manner in which the court seems to excuse any conduct that could be suggestive of harassment as "harmless joking." For example, while the court acknowledged that "there is no way one can defend calling Fitzgerald a dyke or butch," it concluded that these comments were not sufficient to justify a claim, as "the associates who were involved were teasing and joking around, although they were aware of Fitzgerald's discomfort" (*Fitzgerald v. Ford* 2001:45). In other words, the court appears to make a finding of fact (traditionally reserved for the jury) that the associates involved were teasing, despite the acknowledgment that Fitzgerald was uncomfortable with being labeled as a "dyke" or "butch." Further, the court's analysis seems to suggest that when comments are amusing to those who make them, they cannot establish sexual harassment—despite the fact that they are offensive to the listener. When the court further elaborated on the "dyke" and "butch" comments, it noted that no one was attempting to spread the idea that Fitzgerald *actually was a lesbian*—if they were, the court's logic suggests (rather surprisingly) that being incorrectly labeled a lesbian is actionable. The court also notes that during conversations in which Fitzgerald was called a dyke or butch, the remainder of the conversation was "professional and courteous," seeming to indicate that the effects of offensive comments can be somehow diluted or erased when uttered in the midst of an otherwise acceptable conversation.

In considering the sexual comments that were directed at Fitzgerald, the court appears to conclude that a hostile work environment cannot be established unless there is an actual sexual overture to the plaintiff. The court notes that "there is no evidence of [the male associate] attempting to engage in sexual activity of any kind with Fitzgerald, or making any actual sexual advances toward her" (*Fitzgerald v. Ford* 2001:49). One might question this statement, given the e-mail suggesting that Fitzgerald should contact him if her male friend could not "get it done"; the court, however, concludes that the e-mail "was a joking follow-up to the earlier conversation. This again is an example of, at most, crude humor. There is no indication that [the associate] was propositioning Fitzgerald" (*Fitzgerald v. Ford* 2001:50). Throughout this opinion, therefore, the court repeatedly concludes that Fitzgerald's complaints are inadequate to establish a claim of sexual harassment because the comments were made in jest—the court goes so far as to conclude that all of the comments, considered together, were not harassment because the "underlying characteristic of the conversations, remarks and acts complained of, taken as a whole, is that they were in a humorous vein, joking, teasing, *relaxation from the rigors of demanding legal work*" (*Fitzgerald v. Ford* 2001:51, emphasis added). In other words, these comments were simply examples of "boys being boys," and were in keeping with accepted behavior associated with the legal practice.

The Fitzgerald case is a telling example of the challenges a woman attorney faces in employing formal litigation to remedy sexual harassment—not because Fitzgerald should have necessarily won her case based on the facts alleged, but because of the logic employed by the court in granting the law firm's motion for summary judgment. The "legal reasoning" relied on by the court appears to be very much at odds with a woman's experience with sexual harassment. Instead, the opinion reflects an old boys' club mentality that suggests behavior that is demeaning or offensive to a woman should be tolerated, if the men involved believe they are simply joking and need to relieve stress via the degradation of female colleagues.

One tenet of Title VII case law could provide some assistance to women attorneys who are alleging complaints based on "gender harassment," rather than "sexual harassment." Miller (1997) distinguishes between gender harassment and sexual harassment. Sexual harassment encompasses harassment that is of a sexual nature, whereas gender harassment is harassment of an individual because of their gender (i.e., it is not sexual). Legally, sexual harassment law encompasses both of these types of harassment, but the *Fitzgerald* opinion demonstrates that harassment that is blatantly sexual is perhaps seen as more actionable than gender harassment (i.e., being called "butch" or "dyke," being told to dress in a more feminine manner, being labeled as not "aggressive" like male colleagues, etc.). Miller found that men in the armed forces frequently employed covert forms of gender harassment to challenge what they believed was the privileged position of women in the army. These covert types of gender harassment consisted of behaviors such as spreading rumors about women's sex lives, in particular labeling them as a "slut" or "dyke," or claiming that they slept their way to promotion (Miller 1997). Certainly, these types of behaviors are evident in the legal practice, as well as less covert means of harassment.

In *Price Waterhouse v. Hopkins* (1989), the issue of gender harassment was examined directly by the Supreme Court. Hopkins was a senior manager at the Price Waterhouse accounting firm who was denied partnership in the firm.

During her consideration for admission to the partnership, partners repeatedly described her in terms that evidenced their dissatisfaction with her was primarily due to her gender. For instance, one partner asserted that Hopkins was "macho," another claimed that she "overcompensated for being a woman," and still another suggested that she "take a course in charm school" (*Price Waterhouse v. Hopkins* 1989:235). In addition, many of the partners objected to Hopkins' use of profanity, but another partner indicated that this practice was not uncommon and only objectionable in Hopkins because she is a woman. Ultimately, Hopkins' partnership decision was placed on "hold." The partner who explained the decision to Hopkins indicated that she could improve her chances to obtain partnership if she would "walk more femininely, talk more femininely, dress more femininely, wear make-up, have her hair styled, and wear jewelry" (*Price Waterhouse v. Hopkins* 1989:235). The Court determined that "an employer who acts on the basis of a belief that a woman cannot be aggressive, or that she must not be, has acted on the basis of gender" (*Price Waterhouse v. Hopkins* 1989:250). Further, the Court argued that "an employer who objects to aggressiveness in women but whose positions require this trait places women in an intolerable and impermissible Catch-22: out of a job if they behave aggressively and out of a job if they do not. Title VII lifts women out of this bind" (*Price Waterhouse v. Hopkins* 1989:251).

The Court's decision would appear to be tailor-made for women in the legal profession, a male-dominated profession where women have frequently described the very "Catch-22" that the Court prohibits. Nonetheless, women attorneys have not taken advantage of the protection ostensibly offered by this decision. This could be due to a lack of knowledge of the protection Title VII affords those who have been subject to gender discrimination, the knowledge of the difficulty in succeeding in a Title VII case, or a fear of damaging one's career path through a lawsuit. An exploration of discussions in the Greedy Associates community suggests that attorneys in this community have little faith in the ability of the legal system—in which they themselves operate as professional members—to provide relief from employer harms. Their lack of faith is readily communicated to those considering pursuing formal litigation, perhaps serving as a deterrent to the pursuit of such claims.

Greedy Associates Talk about Litigation

Certainly members of the Greedy Associates community do not completely discount the capacity of the legal system to redress harms. When disputes arise, litigation is nearly always introduced as one alternative for obtaining relief. At the same time, however, litigation is rarely ultimately supported as the most viable means to challenge an employer, particularly in gender discrimination matters. Rather, the legal system is generally touted as ineffectual when it comes to correcting for gender disparities. Further, the cost posed to one's career from pursuing a claim against an employer is typically presented as dire within the legal practice, resulting in little encouragement from community members to take formal legal action. This dichotomy, reflected in community members' comments, provides insight into the reasons that some members might reject litigation and consider alternative recourse against their employer.

Attorneys in the community frequently observe that law firms are in violation of antidiscrimination laws and note that women should perhaps employ litigation to challenge these violations. In response to one woman's request for advice over sexual harassment claims, a male attorney advised: "Talk to a lawyer to comply with any statutory deadlines... and walk out with a nice settlement which includes [a] positive reference" (*documentboy*, 30295, 7/03/07). As noted in chapter 4, male attorneys often recommended litigation as a remedy to perceived discrimination.

Further, attorneys in the community seem to view gender discrimination within law firms as widespread. One male attorney, responding to posts about the possible discriminatory handling of promotions at a particular firm, stated,

> There are a LOT of women who could bring down this firm... Bottom line, let the N[ew] Y[ork] L[aw] J[ournal] or W[all] S[treet] J[ournal] take a free walk around, form their own opinion, and call it a day. (*S&S Survivor*, 9187, 12/03/01)

This community member points out that there are a number of women who might have valid legal claims against the firm, when he observes that they could "bring down the firm," and suggests that reporters should investigate the discriminatory and harassing practices at his firm. In response, another male attorney observes that "there are a LOT of women at a LOT of firms (and not just law) that could bring them down" (*Paper Pusher*, 9188, 12/03/01), indicating that sex discrimination is prevalent and women attorneys perhaps could use the law against firms.

Other attorneys imply that litigation might be an advantageous approach when they label behavior as potential violations of legal statutes. For example, one individual concludes that litigation could prove beneficial in handling gender discrimination stating,

> Women who didn't play the game, or weren't pretty enough to be invited, were relegated to a lower status.... Remember also that this has nothing to do with overt sexual relations, although there are many partners that sleep with associates (and summer associates). This sounds very title vii to me. (s*salum*, 8084, 11/07/01)

Labeling this situation as behavior that "sounds very Title VII" is suggestive of a legal violation and the notion that litigation might be appropriate recourse.

These comments, and those like them, suggest that sexual harassment and discrimination is commonplace in law firms, that these behaviors are seen as possible violations of Title VII and other antidiscrimination laws, and that the law itself is viewed as an option in redressing discrimination—women can "bring down" firms through their challenges to discrimination. Although discourse in the community suggests that asserting a claim through formal litigation is a possibility, women are frequently discouraged from actually asserting a claim via a lawsuit.

Perhaps the most common critique litigation receives within the community devolves from attorneys' knowledge that antidiscrimination laws, in practice, are largely ineffectual. Many attorneys are aware of this fact through their own legal practices or the practices of colleagues and friends; others learn of it through interactions occurring within the Web site community. One female attorney in the community contemplated the benefits of litigation asking, "Does anyone know the elements of sexual discrimination in the workplace in New York? I believe that there is sexual discrimination at the law firm I work at, should I bother doing anything about it, or is it a lost cause?" (*angel7*, 14013, 7/02/02). Her comments reflect her interest in pursuing legal action as a possible remedy, since she requests information on the elements of a claim. At the same time, she seems to recognize the weaknesses inherent in a legal action when she asks whether she should "bother" with litigation, as it is perhaps "a lost cause." In response to her request, one attorney is quick to note "I don't know about New York specifically, but I know that in most cases I've seen it's very hard to show sexual discrimination that survives rebuttal ANYWHERE" (*mehitabel*, 14024, 7/03/02). In this peremptory manner, the attorney sets forth what seems to be common knowledge to many attorneys, but few laypersons: sex discrimination and harassment cases are virtually impossible to win and, as a result, there is perhaps little incentive to pursue a claim.

The awareness of the ineffectual nature of antidiscrimination law was voiced by other attorneys, as well, during this particular exchange. One woman attorney explored this problem in depth:

I don't know the exact legal standard, but I do know that especially with law firms unless it's something overt like a physical assault it is almost impossible to do anything about it.... At least under federal law the defense in a discrimination case just has to come up with a plausible alternative reason for their behavior, it doesn't even have to be the real reason. Lawyers are smart they will always come up with some "performance based" reason for the lack of promotion or hiring rather than discrimination and they get former employees to sign non-disclosure agreements. Just think about what happened with lay offs and apply that to all sex discrimination complaints. If it's something personal to you, you may be able to go to a senior partner and get the specific behavior to stop, but don't think that law firms will ever stop doing everything they tell their employment law clients not to do. (*lioness*, 14019, 7/03/02)

This woman expresses skepticism both about law firms' desire to halt discriminatory practices, as well as the ability of the formal litigation process to punish firms for engaging in such behavior. She points out that one would virtually need "physical assault" to establish a case against an employer, particularly a law firm; this observation is supported by the earlier case law analysis within this chapter that suggests the difficulty of establishing a discrimination or harassment claim. Perhaps one of the most striking comments made by this attorney is her suggestion that lawyers at firms believe themselves above the law—that they will not halt the very discriminatory practices that they counsel their clients to avoid.

This sentiment was echoed by a male attorney when discussing the recurring topic of women using their attractiveness to obtain benefits within the practice. He objected to a post by another individual who suggested that sexual favors played a role in advancement in a particular firm, stating "Please, when it comes to the intimate relations between partners and associates and the partner's disdain for federal sexual harassment law, don't ask us to go there" (*S&S Survivor*, 9187, 12/03/01). This attorney dismisses the accusations that female associates use their sexuality to advance and, instead, critiques partners at his firm for engaging in the sexual harassment of women who are not attempting to play sexual games to get ahead. He notes that the partners have "disdain for federal sexual harassment law," once again raising the image of attorneys comfortably operating outside of the law. Similarly, a female attorney observes that "the problem...is with how others a[re] taught to work with [women] and drawing the line between what is, and is not, permissible behavior. Unfortunately, law firms and banks seem to be...exempt from title vii" (*Mistress Stern*, 15745, 11/07/02). There is, therefore, a definite impression by attorneys within the community that law firms tend to operate with a disregard for antidiscrimination law, and that they are also somehow immune from repercussions for their actions. These impressions, coupled with a knowledge of outcomes in gender discrimination cases, could discourage women attorneys in this community from seeking formal legal action. Community members could be particularly discouraged if they come to the Web site seeking advice in connection with a sexual harassment problem and receive feedback such as this that reveals the perceived ineffectiveness of Title VII.

In addition to a lack of faith in the legal system's ability to redress gender discrimination, many of the community members observe that attorneys are fearful of suing their employers due to the damage such an action could inflict on their careers. One board member expressed this concern, stating "Why isn't there a law suit yet? Because everyone knows that an attorney can't get another job at a decent firm if they're suing their previous firm" (*ssalum*, 8663, 11/20/01). Women attorneys who have experienced alleged discrimination are certainly cognizant of the potential consequences of suing their employers. For example, one woman described a claim of pregnancy discrimination, concluding, "I have talked to an attorney and was told I have a pretty good case. I am only a first year attorney though. I worry that suing my first employer may hinder future career opportunities. Should I let them get away with this, or should I sue?" (*esquiremama*, 29635, 01/21/07).

In response to her question, a male attorney queried:

> Is the expected value of the damages you may win (discounting for the risk of losing, and/or expected value of a settlement) worth the risk of even one lost job opportunity? (From now on, every time you interview for a job you don't end up getting, you'll wonder forever—was it my interview, or did they find that case?) On the other hand, if you don't sue, will you wake up every morning (or one morning a month for that matter) and get pissed thinking about this if you don't sue? If you do sue, will it help? What kind of career do you want going forward? This certainly won't stop you from solo or small firm practice. (*JoeChicago*, 29667, 1/24/07)

This attorney recommends that the female attorney engage in a cost/benefit analysis: Is she willing to risk the career costs to satisfy her need to confront her employer? His response suggests that the potential for career repercussions is great. Another male attorney responded in a similar fashion, stating "Sounds like you might have a case and could get some money out of it after a few years... That being said, of course you have to factor in any collateral damage to reputation etc" (*documentboy*, 29663, 1/24/07). Yet another individual responded in a less ambiguous fashion about the career costs of litigation: "If you sue the agency, no agency will hire you for another position. You will be blacklisted. You will not get references. How will this help you find a real job as an attorney? You best bet is to put it behind you and look for a position with a law firm" (*Senior Associate*, 29658, 1/23/07). The woman raising the initial question continued to receive cautions regarding her career (e.g., "As much as I sympathize with your situation I think you would be seriously hurting your career if you sue. Other firms will see you as a trouble-maker" [*msesq02*, 29549, 1/23/07]; "I'd agree about the caution when it comes to the career" [*Gammon1*, 29669, 1/24/07]).

Responding to another complaint regarding gender discrimination, a community member observed that female attorneys are often placed in a difficult predicament when they are faced with a discriminatory work environment:

> [T]he mere existence of [this type of]…environment probably violates title vii (hostile work environment for starters) and in all likelihood eliminates any real possibility of women at the firm being treated in a manner similar to men (the core requirement of title vii). However, here's the problem. If you are a female who was fired, you don't want to bring a[n] EEOC claim—what other law firm in their rightful mind would hire an attorney who files title vii claims against their employer. As there is a glutton of associates in the market due to layoffs and the limited hiring of laterals, this is not a distinction a recently fired associate wants. It's too bad as it sounds as if there are clear violations of title vii going on. (*gameface*, 8062, 11/06/01)

The message that filing an EEOC claim or a lawsuit against one's employer has career consequences is, therefore, repeatedly communicated, indicating that many community members view the filing of a sex discrimination lawsuit as a death knell to one's legal career. As a result, women seeking advice in the community will often encounter discourse suggesting that litigation is a dangerous pursuit.

Due to the ineffectiveness of the legal process itself, the disregard of many law firms for the law, and the dangers posed to one's career as a result of filing a lawsuit, do community members then discourage women from pursuing a rights claim? This predicament is aptly summarized by one male attorney, in recounting a problem posed by a lay-off procedure that appears to be discriminatory:

> Between what I read here, in the press, see at work and hear from friends (in and out of law), whether anyone on here likes it or not, [this firm] may have actually violated some laws besides ruining their reputation. This should really bother many of us because we're in this profession that has drilled ethics into the deepest parts of our brains. Granted, lawyers don't have a great reputation to start with, but if we go by people like you who would rather discuss mundane issues, our profession will just sink. You should realize (I think others do) that there are some serious issues here that extend beyond [this firm] and nobody seems to know what to do about it. The firm made the mistake of mucking up its attrition process so that its public explanation, something that still isn't clear, was exposed as a sham. The more they try to cover up, the more this sounds like they are bursting at the seams with all kinds of real violations. Problem is that nobody knows how to expose a firm as powerful as [this firm] for what they are doing and have done without the threat that [the firm] will ruin their careers (and lives?) forever. (S&S Survivor, 8168, 11/08/01)

This attorney points out the ethical dilemma posed by attorneys ignoring legal violations occurring in a law firm, but at the same time observes that there is no clear way of challenging these practices without endangering one's career. Community members, therefore, seem to view themselves as being in the difficult position of being ethically obligated, and professionally benefited (primarily in the case of women attorneys), to ensure gender equality;

at the same time, they report feeling powerless to use the legal system to change gender practices.

The Greedy Associates community, however, presents a venue by which this problem can perhaps be addressed, as community members are able to articulate informal rights claims, voicing challenges to employer practices and thereby placing pressure on law firms to remedy those practices to avoid damage to their reputation within the legal community. Challenging discrimination online has the important benefit of bypassing the heretofore ineffectual legal system. In addition, attorneys are able to voice complaints without endangering their careers, as they can make their complaints in an anonymous fashion. Members of the Greedy Associates board frequently express gratefulness that the anonymous forum permits them a vehicle for voicing disputes against their employers. As one member stated, "People may be sick of hearing… associates use this board to get the truth out from the partners, but the point about not having other means to hold management accountable is exactly why we ask our questions here" (*S&S Survivor*, 9801, 12/14/01). Similarly, another associate embraced the ability of the community to serve as a mode of expression, contending that "forums like this can hold dishonest partners accountable when we are otherwise powerless" (*shearmanditched*, 9783, 12/14/01). Yet another associate cautioned partners: "You people had better realize that this is not the early 90s and information flows as fast as light" (*Gardener*, 9154, 12/03/01). By raising the ability of the Web site to publicly expose law firm transgressions, the attorney is able to assert a form of power over law firms that was previously unavailable.

The importance of anonymity in this process was articulated by one associate who noted that "anonymous discussion boards are the best thing to show [the partners] our lives without risking [termination]" (*inside*, 15715, 11/06/02). This feeling was echoed by another individual who questioned the hesitancy of partners to identify themselves on the Web site, stating "the G[reedy] A[ssociates] have a reason to stay anonymous, you'll fire us. What's your excuse?" (*Gardener*, 9154, 12/03/01).

Conclusion

Comments by community members reflect both their sense of powerlessness in challenging partners through means such as formal litigation, as well as the empowerment provided by the cover of anonymity that accompanies the Web site community. Although their comments indicate a desire to avoid direct confrontation with their employers in the formal legal system, they also reflect a desire to confront and challenge current working conditions.

Does the law have any role to play in community members' attempts to challenge gender discrimination? Scheingold (1974) observes that although litigation itself perhaps effects little change, judicial decisions serve to alter the expectations and self-conceptions of the disadvantaged, permitting the creation of a new sense of collective identity that can benefit mobilization efforts. He contends, therefore, that the idea that the litigation process itself can exact change is a myth, but calling on litigation results can be useful as part of political mobilization efforts. Although attorneys in the Internet community might articulate little benefit in the formal litigation process, they do reference rights awarded under both Title VII and its subsequent case law. Community members might, therefore, incur a benefit through their ability to organize and make demands under a legally established claim to a right—the right not to experience gender discrimination. In the next chapter, I explore the potential power of such rights discourse, examining whether attorneys within the community might be able to utilize legal discourse, rather than formal litigation, to challenge gender inequality. When disputes are framed in terms of "rights" that have been violated, they gain a greater air of legitimacy. As a result, these rights claims bring more pressure to bear on the opposing party. Further, employing legal discourse to challenge gender inequality could prove more advantageous than pursuing formal litigation, as it would be considerably less costly. In addition, and perhaps more importantly, the Internet discussion boards allow attorneys to engage in rights discourse under the cover of anonymity, thereby aiding them in avoiding the career costs associated with litigation.

6

Lawyers Using Legal Discourse to Challenge Gender Discrimination

With the perceived failure of litigation to challenge gender inequality in the legal practice, one could argue that the law itself is of no utility in bringing about change for women attorneys. Nonetheless, the use of rights and legal discourse might still prove an effective tool for women lawyers. A number of scholars have explored the power of rights discourse to both mobilize actual legal actions and to simply rally groups to push for change. By calling on codified law and concepts of "natural law," groups are able to apply pressure for change. The use of rights discourse might, in fact, prove better adapted to the needs of women attorneys when such discourse is used in an Internet community. The Internet has been viewed as a means by which individuals can generate counterhegemonic discourse (Warf and Grimes 1997); this is particularly true for those who have been unable to articulate their demands openly offline.

Associate attorneys in general, as well as women associates in particular, certainly fall into this category of individuals; voicing claims through litigation has been heretofore ineffective, and making claims either formally or informally could endanger their careers. As a result, the Greedy Associates community might prove an effective ground for counterhegemonic discourse regarding definitions and understandings of gender inequality and discrimination. By employing rights and legal discourse in the community, community members are able to challenge employer practices under the shelter of anonymity. As examined in this chapter, attorneys' use of legal discourse both embraces formal understandings of gender discrimination and introduces new, broader concepts of discrimination. By using legal discourse within the community to label employer behavior as discriminatory, community members are able to bring pressure to bear on employers, even in situations where employer actions fall outside the realm of legally recognized prohibited behavior.

Using Rights Discourse to Effect Change

Many view the law as a powerful force for change, exemplified by the civil rights movement in which repeated appeals to the law (as opposed to simply the existence of the law on the books) assisted in bringing about victories for minority groups. Due to this perceived entitlement to a kind of "justice" present in natural law, the oppressed often call upon the law in attempts to challenge both intolerance and oppression. Karst (1989:1) notes that "equality has been a rallying cry" in the United States that not only serves to unite the oppressed, but also provides a basis for legal challenge to effectuate change. He observes that Americans appear to have great faith in the ability of the law to enforce notions of egalitarianism.

Americans' invocation of the language of equality or legal rights when challenging those in power suggests that individuals' understandings of the way law works can be as important, or perhaps more important, as the law on the books if such understanding is used to mobilize the oppressed (Marshall and Barclay 2003). Law is mobilized when a desire is transformed into a demand as an assertion of rights (McCann 1994); this demand parallels the claiming stage of the dispute process (Felstiner, Abel, and Sarat 1980–1981). Assertions of rights can "give rise to rights consciousness so that individuals and groups may imagine and act in light of rights that have not been formally recognized or enforced" (McCann 1994:7; Marshall and Barclay 2003). Legal consciousness (or rights consciousness), therefore, "refers to the ongoing, dynamic process of constructing one's understanding of, and relationship to, the social world through use of legal conventions and discourses" (McCann 1994:7). The legal consciousness of both laypersons and lawyers might be based on perceptions of the law, rather than the reality of it; nonetheless, this consciousness is an integral component in the process of making a claim for change.

The efficacy of using rights discourse as a tool for change is oft debated. Critical legal scholars contend that equality cannot be achieved through the law, arguing that even engaging in rights discourse is inconsistent with the goal of social change. Although legal victories can temporarily energize a social movement, critical legal scholars argue that reliance on legal remedies and the assertion of rights ultimately results in the legitimization of existing inequalities and repression (Crenshaw 1995; Altman 1990; Schneider 1990). This legitimization occurs because, when rights discourse is employed, the social movement of the disadvantaged is organized "according to the law's boundaries and, in turn, [is] bound by its conceptual limitations"

(Crenshaw 1995:108). As a result, the legitimacy of the current social order is never truly challenged because the oppressed choose to operate within their oppressor's system of law. Thus, when women attempt to challenge gender inequality through the use of legal discourse, they must do so by appealing to legal notions steeped in the male dominance of the legal system. As previously discussed, those who write the laws, argue the cases, and interpret the laws have been, and remain, predominantly male (Baer 1999; Rhode 2001). Critical legal scholars, therefore, maintain that women who draw upon rights discourse are legitimating the male hierarchy by choosing to operate within the legal system.

Rights discourse not only legitimates the legal system of the oppressors, but Tushnet (1984) contends that it fails to effect change because rights discourse limits the ability of its users to step back and truly examine the current problem; instead, the "real demands, experiences, and concerns" of the oppressed are absorbed into a "vacuous and indeterminate discourse" (Crenshaw 1995:109, citing Tushnet 1984). As a result, the oppressed lose touch with their original objectives as they attempt to fit their problems into a rights category. Similarly, legal doctrines permit multiple interpretations, resulting in the ability to twist the law to fit one's own particular perspective (Altman 1990; Unger 1989). Given the malleability of the law, critical legal scholars argue that it is difficult for individuals to truly mobilize behind a claim of rights, since their oppressors can turn the same rights claim against the oppressed. The language of law is too easily manipulated to the will of the one who wields it, and the interpretation of those with the most power is likely to triumph. The ability to twist the law in this manner leads some to the difficult conclusion that "because everything can be defended, nothing can" (Unger 1989:8), resulting in the law serving little or no utility for effecting change. Despite these noted weaknesses, many advocate the use of rights discourse to challenge oppression. Proponents of liberal legal and political philosophy contend that when the law is applied faithfully by the government, the dominant values of individual liberty will prevail (Altman 1990). Altman (1990) argues that liberalism can accommodate the critical legal scholars' critiques, contending that although law cannot serve as the sole recourse for the oppressed, the law can be employed as a significant resource for protecting people from intolerance and oppression.

Crenshaw (1995), for instance, acknowledges the critical legal scholars' arguments that rights rhetoric is of limited usefulness in effecting change. Nonetheless, Crenshaw contends that the critical legal scholars' view fails to consider the powerful role that rights discourse has played in social movements, such as the manner in which the civil rights movement mobilized minorities and assisted in creating new demands for rights. Crenshaw argues that by discrediting the utility of rights discourse, the critical legal scholars might unintentionally disempower the oppressed by removing this method of challenging the dominant culture. Specifically, critical legal scholars deconstruct rights discourse, yet offer no alternative strategy for producing change (Crenshaw 1995; Altman 1990).

Crenshaw (1995) and Altman (1990) posit that there is no alternative strategy and, as a result, the oppressed should turn to the law as a method for challenging the dominant social order. Schneider (1990) supports this viewpoint, contending that the critical legal scholars focus only on the limits of rights, rather than the possibilities offered by rights discourse. She emphasizes that rights discourse can affirm human values, enhance political growth, and assist in the development of a collective identity; all of these elements can prove invaluable to a political struggle.

How, then, can a claim to right be transformed into an effective weapon in a political movement? Rights discourse can be a particularly effective tool for the disadvantaged, as such discourse appeals to the dominant ideology and, as a result, is more likely to be accepted as legitimate (Crenshaw 1995). One manner of producing change, therefore, is to expose a contradiction between the dominant ideology (such as the American notion of equality) and reality (the fact that inequality exists). By utilizing rights discourse, "powerless people can sometimes trigger...a crisis by challenging an institution internally, that is, by using its own logic against it" (Crenshaw 1995:111). When such a discrepancy is exposed, the damage to the dominant ideology can be of such a nature that the dominant group will desire to repair the inequality to maintain its vision of equality (Crenshaw 1995). As a result, rights discourse can be an effective mode of change because it calls upon the dominant ideology of equality and natural rights and can elicit a desire to correct situations contrary to these notions.

Scheingold (1974) notes that the rhetoric of rights plays an important role in political discourse, as it brings values embodied in the Constitution into politics. Individuals engaged in mobilization efforts often "speak in terms of rights that are violated, obligations unfulfilled, punishment of the guilty, vindication of the innocent" (Scheingold 1974:44). Even when a right has not been authoritatively established by the judicial or legislative process, an assertion of rights is "not simply empty rhetoric" (Scheingold

1974:44–45). Rights rhetoric calls on moral norms, compelling the listener to support and defend the cause to support and defend the accompanying moral norm. Mobilization efforts are thereby "made possible by the presence of rights in American society" (Scheingold 1974:83). Once again, whether the right has been recognized by the legislative or judicial system is unimportant; the belief system of rights influences social change. The success of a rights assertion lies more in its association with social justice than in its having been recognized by an authority as protected. Rights discourse can be a powerful weapon for the disadvantaged; "legal and constitutional processes might not be able to neutralize power relationships," but "the authoritative declaration of a right can be viewed as the beginning of a political process in which power relationships loom large and immediate" (Scheingold 1974:85).

In the case of gender inequality in the legal profession, women attorneys are dealing not necessarily with making changes within American society as a whole, but within the law firm environment. As the notion of rights is engrained within the legal practice, perhaps mobilization through the use of rights discourse is nowhere more appropriate than in the legal practice, where attorneys might be able to bring about change by using the very logic of the legal system against itself.

As noted by Marshall and Barclay (2003), one's view of whether the law can serve as a successful tool for change depends in part on one's own experiences with the law, perceptions of the law, and hopes for what the law should be. Ewick and Silbey (1998) observe that individuals typically relate to the law in one of three manners: they are before the law (awed by its majesty and legitimacy); with the law (utilizing it when it favors them, and treating it like a game); or against the law (cynical and distrustful of its implementation). The particular mode of legal consciousness one adopts tends to be associated with social status, with those who are less powerful tending to be "against the law." In this regard, Nielsen (2000) found that women, who were more likely to experience harassment on the street, were less supportive of legislation prohibiting this very harassment. Similarly, women in the legal community might bear a less optimistic view of the utility of legal discourse for bringing about change. It is doubtless that the particular legal consciousness of the members of the Web site community plays an important role in determining whether they choose to mobilize the law to challenge inequality, or whether they view the law as an ineffective tool for change.

Legal Mobilization in the Greedy Associates Community

Legal mobilization can be an important factor in producing change, especially if utilized during the movement-building stage (McCann 1994). The Greedy Associates community might provide a fertile environment for movement-building to occur through legal mobilization. As examined in chapter 4, members of the community are able to exchange information and experiences that assist one another through the dispute process. Once the claiming process is reached, community members can pursue a formal lawsuit or can utilize rights discourse to garner support within the community for their claim and perhaps prompt a response from their employers.

Indeed, other employees have utilized computer networks to challenge employer practices (see discussion in chapter 2, citing Warf and Grimes 1997; Wellman et al. 1996; Pliskin and Romm 1994; Zuboff 1988). Just as in other employee movements initiated on the Internet, the Greedy Associates community could prove a successful means by which to challenge employer practices. Although members of the Web community rarely mention a definite intent to sue their employers, they do engage in rights discourse, both through the suggestion of legal action and through challenging law firms to respond to their claims. The following sections analyze some examples of the utilization of rights discourse in the Web community, providing support for the notion that the Web community could serve as a medium for attorneys to elicit change in gender relations within the legal practice.

Greedy Associates Using Rights Discourse to Challenge Working Conditions

The Greedy Associates members frequently call upon rights discourse in the process of challenging working conditions in general, as well as gender inequality in particular. The fact that the board, initially created as a forum to discuss firm salary hikes, has morphed into a place in which associates assert rights claims regarding working conditions bodes well for the prospect of women attorneys using the board to challenge gender discrimination.

One of the most common complaints made by attorneys is that working conditions are incompatible with maintaining a normal family and social life. Hours are long, the pressure is high, and many associates report feeling underappreciated. Associates at the Greedy Associate Web site frequently assert that they have a "right" to better working conditions, despite their sizeable monetary compensation.

One individual suggested that associates should "grin and bear it," rather than complain of working conditions, because they are well-compensated for their troubles (*dvadar*, 8188, 11/08/01). Another attorney quickly lashed back, questioning "Are you implying that associates at biglaw firms should be grateful for the job they have and the pay they get, regardless of conditions. I know we're not working in a coal mine but don't you think that employees in an industry have the right to demand better pay and better conditions?" (*Paper Pusher*, 8197, 11/08/01). Similarly, another attorney bemoans the lifestyle difficulties created by long hours and billable hour requirements, stating

> firms...are never truthful enough about the difficult choices that one is compelled to make between having a normal and meaningful life and being a highly prized contributor to the firm. Yes of course, one does not get paid the big bucks for nothing in return, but how much is enough.... Humane working conditions (generously defined) do not have to be so hopelessly at odds with big bucks. (*corporate diva*, 5724, 7/26/01)

The attorney implies that law firms misrepresent working conditions, and they lack "humane working conditions," thereby suggesting that there is some natural right to humane conditions that is not currently being met in the legal field.

The issue of layoffs within law firms created a great deal of controversy in the board community, as layoffs were uncommon in the legal field until recent years. In response to allegations that layoffs were implemented in an unfair manner, a board member stated,

> Not sure what [the firm's] current policy is on managing poor performers and denying retention bonuses,

but...listening to the stories (here, from friends and in the papers) of how random lay-offs were, the so-called "under performers" probably do have a right to more than [the firm] is giving if the firm didn't follow its policies. They are more likely entitled to the "retention" bonuses if the lay-offs were due to mismanagement and over-hiring because (can they really be this dumb) the layoffs were a product of the success of the bonus program. How can it make sense to say to an associate, "we'll pay you to forego other opportunities" and then say "because you didn't leave, we're cutting you and you have no right to the bonus that kept you here?" This seems so obvious that I bet anyone without a JD (a juror) would see the injustice. (*ssalum*, 8353, 11/14/01)

This attorney asserts a claim against the law firm on behalf of the terminated associates, relying upon legal discourse and logic, as well as claims of rights and entitlement. The attorney claims that terminated employees perhaps have a right, or are entitled, to additional payment, suggesting a legal obligation; he or she then drives home the point by indicating that a juror would be able to recognize the rights violations that occurred. Another attorney asserted that law firms violated a quasi-legal obligation to employees by engaging in layoffs at all, arguing that

Many of these firms (especially in the last few years) just about promised associates job security. Don't you think that these layoffs are to some extent a breach of faith (of course it wasn't contractual or otherwise enforcable). Don't you think that there was an understanding at big-law firms, a sort of implied quid pro quo. I always thought that if you are a biglaw associate and you bust your ass, then although you might not make partner, you will still have job security until you get passed over (barring some egregious behavior). (*Paper Pusher*, 8197, 11/08/01)

This attorney readily acknowledged that there was no "contractual" or "enforceable" obligation between the law firms and the associates who were the victims of lay-offs. Nonetheless, the individual suggests that there was an "implied quid pro quo" and that the firm engaged in a "breach of faith"—the phrasing definitely connoting a legal claim. The attorney has, therefore, both denied the existence of a formal right and, simultaneously, used legal language to assert that very right.

Attorneys in the community seem to be more reluctant to use legal discourse to demand a remedy for claims connected with gender inequality; this hesitancy is perhaps due to a perception that the law, in general, has been inef-fectual in assisting women in dealing with gender discrim-ination and harassment issues. Quinn (2000) observes that women are often hesitant not only to use legal discourse to demand a remedy for sexual harassment, but they also fail to label sexual harassment as "sexual harassment." When women do not use legal terminology to name their harm, Quinn argues that they disempower the law, both as a tool to seek a remedy and as a discursive power. The law has discursive power, regardless of whether or not a claim for remedy is made; by labeling an action as "sexual harassment," a woman can call upon the power of the law to cause the action to cease, even if she never files a formal complaint (Quinn 2000). Whether the law is being used as a discursive tool, or as a formal method of pursuing a remedy, it is important that the individual name the harm in legal terms. If one fails to do so, "the law is immobilized both ideologically and instrumentally" (Quinn 2000:1155). Consequently, if attorneys are reluctant to label gender inequality in legal terms, the law cannot be used in its dis-cursive form to challenge the inequality.

When examining the use of legal discourse in the Greedy Associates community, therefore, it becomes important to determine whether attorneys use legal terms both in identifying harms, as well as in making a claim for remedy. When discussing gender issues, community members are much more likely to use legal discourse when labeling a harm, than in demanding a right. As recounted in chapter 4, one female attorney announced to community members: "I am facing a sexual harassment problem" (*bostonlawgirl*, 20465; 7/08/04). Similarly, another attorney stated, "So any guesses which... firm can't seem to figure out the definition of 'sexual harassment'? Apparently the higher-ups need to meet about it, while the litigators just practice it, with a little comment here, a little picture there, a lot of trouble" (*KHHInsider*, 25167, 7/08/05). It is important to recognize that by merely calling inappropriate behavior "sexual harassment," community members are using legal discourse to challenge the behavior. When an offense is characterized by legal terminology, it imbues the claim with legal authority and places pressure on the offender to transform his or her behavior; this is true, regardless of whether a formal claim for remedy is made (Quinn 2000).

At times, attorneys take this process a step further by not simply using legal terminology to label a harm, but in assessing the legality of particular behavior. For instance, a male attorney argued that one woman's experiences with her employer might not be harassment claiming "just because you subjectively feel uncomfortable doesn't make it sexual harassment" (*eyestrain*, 20466, 07/08/04). In response, another attorney states,

WRONG. Note the first word of the EEOC's definition of sexual harassment: "*Unwelcome* sexual

advances...constitutes sexual harassment when submis-
sion to or rejection of this conduct explicitly or implicitly
affects an individual's employment, unreasonably inter-
feres with an individual's work performance or creates
an intimidating, hostile or offensive work environment."
Yes, there is an objective element to consider, but what
you said is just wrong. (*boxer*, 20471, 7/08/04)

This exchange indicates the easy manner by which attorneys fall into the use of legal discourse in discussing
workplace issues. The first individual attempts to make a
blanket legal statement in assessing how a woman should
proceed in dealing with harassing behavior. Note that
this is different than a layperson's argument of what does
or does not constitute sexual harassment; the attorney is
clearly referring to the necessary elements to establish a
sexual harassment *claim*, rather than simply offering an
opinion about whether the behavior should be generally
considered to be harassing. In response, another attorney
refers to a specific right contained on the books, when he
or she cites a portion of the EEOC guidelines on harassment. Engaging in a debate concerning the legality of the
alleged behavior is an important method of establishing
the legitimacy of a complaint and, thereby, placing pressure on an employer to provide a remedy.

In one of the discussions concerning the retention of
attractive female associates with poor work records, one
male attorney contended "what is being described...is
mean spirited, and actionable by the ["unattractive"]
woman if she so chooses" (*roveresq*, 8050, 11/06/01). This
observation prompted a debate among the community
members concerning whether a cause of action exists
when women who are not considered attractive, or do
not use their attractiveness to play sexual "games" with

partners, are terminated. One attorney asserted that "the mere existence of a gamey environment probably violates Title VII...and in all likelihood eliminates any real possibility of women at the firm being treated in a manner similar to men" (*gameface*, 8062, 11/06/01). The attorney goes on, however, to state that an actual lawsuit would likely fail and/or damage an attorney's career, but nonetheless reemphasizes that "it sounds as if there is [*sic*] clear violations of Title VII going on" (*gameface*, 8062, 11/06/01). Once again, therefore, the intent of many of the attorneys in analyzing whether a valid legal claim exists appears to be less about encouraging litigation, than about determining whether a situation can be legitimately labeled as a rights violation. The power in these exchanges lies more in the ability to cast suspicion on the legality of a firm's behavior, and perhaps prompt a response, than in encouraging a lawsuit.

Similarly, when attorneys describe situations that they claim "sound like" Title VII violations (e.g., *ssalum*, 8084, 11/07/01; *Mistress Stern*, 15745, 11/07/02), their words have the dual function of perhaps suggesting that litigation be pursued, as well as framing the employer's behavior in terms of the violation of a right. In other words, even if litigation is never pursued (as is likely the case), and even if the author never considers litigation a viable option, the mere labeling of behavior as a "Title VII violation" has a power unto itself. A law firm has been described to the legal community as a law violator and, whether or not an actual law has been violated, pressure is placed on the firm to respond in some manner to the accusation. One male attorney, in fact, makes note of this reality, contending that the firm involved in the questionable layoff practices "HAS become the talk of the legal associate and student community and the taint will last for years to come" (*S&S Survivor*, 7967, 11/05/01). Another individual, directing a response to a partner of the same firm, voiced a similar observation, stating

> Now a day doesn't pass when I don't hear something about how this firm sucks, how I bet wrong in law school (I had "other options"), how embarrassed I must be after last year [when the terminations occurred]....So go back to working with our defunct IT department to figure out who is really on this board and get off our backs. Or better yet, why don't you try to restore some decency to this firm. Don't blame greedyassociates for [the firm's] problems. (*voice from hell*, 11831, 03/19/02)

This message reveals the manner in which critiques of the legality of a firm's behaviors can serve to damage the firm's reputation in the legal community, as well as the power of the legal discourse to prompt exchanges between partners and associates. In this message, the associate is able to deflect the alleged partner's accusations that the Web site community is responsible for the firm's poor reputation, and instead assert that the firm itself must remedy the damage it has inflicted on its own reputation.

The above examples demonstrate that members of the Greedy Associates community use rights discourse and legal language to describe rights violations, make demands for remedies, and to imply an obligation to challenge discrimination. The use of rights and legal discourse in all of these manners can place pressure on an employer to investigate, respond to, and perhaps remedy behaviors. Further, the use of the Web community for this type of interaction has become so commonplace that at times such discourse dominates the board, as opposed to conversations regarding law firm salaries. The Web site, therefore, shows promise as a forum in which attorneys can assert rights claims against law firms and, perhaps, prompt change in gender relations.

In addition to challenging gender discrimination directly, community members use legal discourse in at least two additional manners that demonstrate promise for the ability of the community to effect change. Legal discourse has been used in discussing the possibility of establishing a labor union to protect attorney rights; the existence of a union could provide additional protection to women challenging gender discrimination. In addition, community members have employed legal discourse when asserting their right to voice grievances in the Web site community, demonstrating a knowledge of the importance of this community in challenging working conditions. Both of these instances are explored, in the following text, to better evaluate the potential for the community to impact the legal practice.

Greedy Associates Use Legal Discourse in Collective Mobilization Efforts

In 2001, many community members began to report that employers were prohibiting their participation in the Greedy Associates community, with a varied list of penalties that could be incurred for violations of these prohibitions. Members of the community were outraged at reports of law firm "censorship" of the Web site content and, in response, they sought methods of protecting their right to participate in the community for the purpose of challenging working conditions and law firm actions. The talk quickly focused on employees' rights to unite against their employer, be it in an online environment or otherwise.

Talk of the right to collective mobilization began when one attorney noted that "employees do have the right, under the National Labor Relations Act, to communicate with one another for the purpose of 'mutual aid and protection' and for the purpose of organizing collective action" (*Afterburn*, 8090, 11/07/01). After asserting the existence of a legal right that could be applicable, the attorney went on to assess the merits of a Natural Labor Relations Act (NLRA) claim to a right to organize at the Web site community:

> If you are using this board to communicate with fellow...employees to discuss your working conditions, it is very questionable whether [the firm] can punish associates, or threaten to punish associates, for using it. [The firm] may be committing an unfair labor practice under the NLRA (which applies to both unionized and non-unionized employees). A key aspect is that the protection generally applies only to speech related to protecting the employees as a group, not to your own personal complaints or disputes. (*Afterburn*, 8090, 11/07/01)

By asserting a right, referencing the NLRA, and framing his or her analysis in legal language, the board member created an air of legitimacy that other board members were quick to rally behind. One male attorney responded

> So, if the firm is communicating either poorly, or maybe even deceptively, about the course and conduct of its firings, and the firm is using its power to leverage associates into silence, then THEY risk violating a federal regulation if they instruct current and fired associates from using

the Internet to obtain accurate data? Interesting. I would think that the firm's comp. & benefits group would know about this. If, in fact, senior partners have told associates to stay off of this board (which they have), they should probably retract that statement, don't you think? (*S&S Survivor*, 8092, 11/07/01)

This attorney's response clearly identifies an injury and a claim of right against the law firm, and then takes the process a step further by making a fairly precise demand of the firm, that is, that they retract their prohibition of communication on the Web site. Through the use of legal discourse, the individual is able to exert pressure on the firm, an entity that he or she readily acknowledges maintains power over associates.

Recognizing this shift in the power structure, the notion of "workers' rights" was readily embraced by other board members who sought to explore the extent to which they could utilize the notion of employee rights to exert pressure on law firms. One male attorney questioned, "Without an official union, do associates have the right to demand a meeting of all those that were fired so that they can share their mutual stories and maybe get to the bottom of this?" (*S&S Survivor*, 8093, 11/07/01). Although one attorney responded that employees have no "right to demand a meeting," he or she encouraged collective action by stating that the firms "can't stop you from meeting or communicating with those people on non-work time" (*Afterburn*, 8094, 11/07/01). In this manner, community members began to explore the notion of communicating online for the purposes of collective action.

As a result of this discussion, the idea of collective action in the form of unionization was raised within the community. One male attorney, recognizing that the NLRA permits a shift in the power structure between employer and employee, implored,

> if only associates communicated together for their mutual benefit. if only they would organize and realize what wage slaves they actually are. there is a sceptre [sic] haunting the law firms and that sceptre is union. (ishbaal, 8091, 11/07/01)

By encouraging associates to take advantage of the legal rights available to unionized employees, this community member uses the notion of legal rights in an attempt to compel collective action.

The idea of unionization once again surfaced in the online community at a later date, when one board member defended the idea that the board should be used to vent grievances against employers by saying, "Well, this and other anonymous discussion boards are the best thing to show them our lives without risking [termination], unless we unionize" (inside, 15715, 11/06/02). Board members immediately took up the notion of unionization, with one male attorney wondering "why there aren't more lawyers in unions, especially those that work at union busting Firms" (laborguy, 15788, 11/08/02). Possible explanations for the lack of unions, suggested another attorney, include

> (1) the associates will not pay dues for professional memberships that they cannot get reimbursed by the firm; and (2) we already have healthcare, flextime and high salaries without collective bargaining. Also, while that 3 month notice associates are being given is not long enough to find a replacement job (and market used to be 6) it is much better than anything your secretary could get, unionized or not. (ElaborateHoax, 15790, 11/08/02)

This individual, therefore, seemed to believe that unions could provide attorneys with no advantages because attorneys already possess decent benefits; he or she fails, however, to acknowledge that the existence of numerous complaints regarding working conditions are issues that a union could assist in addressing. Recognizing this fact, another community member states,

> i see the hurdles to unionizing, but i don't hear you saying that it [*sic*] off the table…the pay and benefits thing doesn't work for me as an exclusion or else who [*sic*] could those with good benefits and near equal pay (commercial pilots, engineers, plumbers, etc.) unionize. i can see outrage from the public who do not understand what has become of the legal profession, but if they knew the realities of how the economic interests have overtaken ethical beliefs resulting in overall higher costs to the u.s. gdp, i think that, as associates with principle, we could woo them to our side. (*inside*, 15798, 11/08/02)

This board member claims in his or her post that associates can exact change in their working conditions by unionizing and suggests that the community could influence the public to support the notion of a union for lawyers through exposure of current working conditions.

Other individuals suggest that a union is unnecessary because the state bar serves, or can serve, a similar purpose. "Perhaps rather than a union," argued one attorney, "what we need is for the N[ew] Y[ork] S[tate] B[ar] to run more of a closed shop in this state, and restrict the ability of cheap foreign labor to undercut N[ew] Y[ork] S[tate] qualified JDs" (*ElaborateHoax*, 15790, 11/08/02). Another attorney agreed that the bar can act as a union, arguing that "there's an element of unionization going on: but for the monopoly of the bar, there is no reason why a system bypassing law school is less effective: law firms hire college grads and train them to practice law, perhaps incurring more costs for formal training to make up for the lack of law school, and pay a much lower salary and bill at a lower rate" (*hervelino*, 15991, 11/19/02). In other words, he or she claims that the very existence of state bars regulating the field of law provides some job security to attorneys since specialized training is required to practice law.

The idea that bar associations can serve the same function as a union, however, was rejected by other board members who argued that such associations cannot protect the interests of associates when partners are members of and retain much of the power in the bar. "The bar associations," argues one board member, "are held in the pockets of those that favor the status quo, so i don't see that as effective" (*inside*, 15798, 11/08/02). Another individual agreed that the bar provides some job protection, but contends that "it's not a very effective union when the bosses are members too" (*Jor*, 15994, 11/19/02). The notion that the benefits of unions are special and could serve as a vehicle for change within law firms seemed to prevail against counter arguments.

By engaging in the debate over unionization and labor rights, community members effectively employ legal discourse in the discussion of employee rights, violations of those rights, and methods to ensure protection of employee rights. Engaging in these very discussions could compel action on part of law firms, as employers are fearful of the implications of unionization. In addition, however, these discussions serve to rally community members around the notion of uniting to challenge employer practices. Whether an attorney "union" ever materializes or gains support from these debates is of less importance, perhaps, than the discourse suggesting that legal rights might exist that would provide employees with power over their employers. In a time when law firms seem to be largely "immune" from antidiscrimination law, this discourse can serve an important function in uniting and mobilizing attorneys to challenge unfair practices, including gender discrimination.

Greedy Associates Use Legal Discourse to Assert the Right to Use Legal Discourse

Unionization was not the only, or even the first, response to reports of employer "censorship" of the Greedy Associates Web site. Faced with restrictions on their ability to post messages about their firms, attorneys in the community jumped to the apparently instinctual conclusion that they must have a *right* to engage in such activity, labeling the firms' prohibitions as "censorship" and violations of First Amendment rights. One attorney implored "isn't there a 1st amendment thing so long as I don't do it from within the building? Does this bother anyone?" (*S&S Survivor,* 8088, 11/07/01). Another responded in horror, "ARE YOU KIDDING???!!!! This is terrible. Is [the firm] that afraid of the truth.... Definitely a free speech issue, although you can continue to write whatever you want, but I suppose they can just fire you" (*randomassociate,* 8100, 11/07/01). Notably, this attorney begins by expressing shock at the firms' actions and readily invokes the notion of free speech, but then admits that the firm can fire individuals if they operate in violation of the firm's orders.

The attorney's ultimate conclusion that firms have the "right" to terminate employees who violate no-posting rules is perhaps the more realistic of the two responses to law firm "censorship." One attorney derided those calling on the First Amendment, stating "you went to law school? you only have 1st amendment rights for prior restraint by gov't. say what you want where you want, but there may be consequences" (*ishbaal*, 8089, 11/07/01). This attorney is certainly correct. After an employee was terminated by his employer for maintaining a Web site with questionable content, Lewis Maltby, director of the American Civil Liberties Union's Workplace Rights office, explained that the First Amendment protects an individual's right to present his or her opinion on a Web site but does not prevent a private employer from terminating the employee due to the Web site content (Silberman 1998). Maltby observed, "You should take a passport when you enter the private sector, because you leave your rights as an American citizen behind. Once you go into the private sector, the Constitution doesn't exist. You have no constitutional rights."[1]

Nonetheless, attorneys who have been well-trained in the law instinctively called on the First Amendment when faced with limitations placed upon their speech by law firms. Further, another invoked the First Amendment's reference to freedom of association, claiming that it afforded attorneys protection against law firm attacks on Web site posting:

> Thanks G[reedy] A[ssociates], this makes the board more than a pure gossip arena, more like the information age water cooler. Damn, if only law firms could figure out how to get around that First Amendment freedom of association loophole. (*shearmanditched*, 9783, 12/14/01)

This reliance upon rights discourse is a strong enough force that even attorneys who know of the law's inability to equalize all playing grounds will resort to imagined legal protection in the face of oppression. Scheingold (1974) and Crenshaw (1995) both acknowledge that legal discourse can be a powerful mode for change, even when the rights referenced have not been authoritatively established by the legislative or judicial system. The ability to argue for rights where none exist is important in seeking to effect social change; if attorneys are to be successful in using legal discourse on behalf of women attorneys, they must be able to refer to both legally recognized rights (notions of equality and antidiscrimination), as well as rights that have yet to be placed into formal law.

In addition, the debates that erupted over the "censorship" issue demonstrate a strong commitment to the community as a forum to voice complaints against employers, and perhaps compel a response. One attorney noted the power of the Web site in providing a community that allows attorneys to challenge partners' decisions, such as this one, stating that "forums like this can hold dishonest partners accountable when we are otherwise powerless" (*shearmanditched*, 9783, 12/14/01). In particular, attorneys posting at the Web site are able to use the power of legal discourse in an attempt to publicize disfavored firm practices, such as gender discrimination and sexual harassment, and perhaps effectuate change.

7

Conclusion

Interactions in the Greedy Associates community present an opportunity for attorneys to receive assistance in progressing through the dispute process and perhaps reaching a decision to assert a rights claim. Attorneys might enter the community before identifying an injury or assigning blame for the injury; by engaging in an exchange with other attorneys who share legal knowledge and experience with the law firm culture, these individuals can be aided in their navigation of a dispute. Concomitantly, attorneys can be stymied in their ability to assert a claim when they encounter discouraging discourse regarding litigating claims. Superior knowledge regarding the inefficacy of legal outcomes, as well as enhanced career costs to litigation, are articulated in a manner that can lead community members to conclude that the law is an ineffectual remedy to complaints of gender discrimination. Nonetheless, the community's unique nesting in a legal context encourages the use of legal discourse in challenging employer discrimination. The use of legal discourse in an anonymous forum has potential for providing attorneys with a powerful tool for subverting power relations in law firms and reconstituting current definitions of discrimination.

The ability of legal discourse in the community to generate an offline effect in remedying gender inequities can perhaps best be understood through an analysis of the manner in which the law, culture, and environment work in tandem to influence rights claims (McEvoy 2005). Cultural and institutional norms both within and outside of the legal profession play a role in generating the current climate within the legal practice. A challenge to gender discrimination must, therefore, incorporate a consideration of all of its sources. As depicted by figure 7.1, women's claims to the right of a discrimination and harassment-free workplace are affected by the interaction of (1) judicial interpretations of the law, (2) law firm organizational management and culture, (3) the experiences of associate attorneys, and (4) the way in which associate experiences are differentiated by gender.

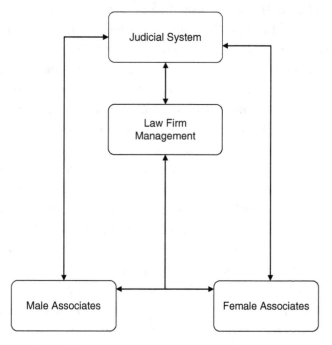

Figure 7.1 Multilevel interactions involved in attorneys' claims to rights.

At all of these levels, the definition of what constitutes prohibited gender discrimination is formed and reinforced in everyday practices of the legal system and in organizational practices. The interaction of understandings of gender and gender relations at these levels serves to discourage discrimination and harassment claims by women lawyers, as well as to encourage the continuation of the status quo. Consequently, this concluding chapter examines the manner in which these separate forces intermingle to create obstacles to rights claims, as well as the way in which employing legal discourse in the Greedy Associates community provides a method of subverting this process. Ultimately, through the use of legal discourse in the Greedy Associates community, attorneys can perhaps challenge existing understandings of discrimination and take a step toward altering gender relations within the legal practice.

Management and Organizational Culture Discourage Rights Claims

It is typically the organization itself that is deemed responsible for the creation of an unfriendly working environment, as well as for creating obstacles to challenging that environment. This understanding is reflected in antidiscrimination law, which purports to hold the employer liable for harms resulting from discrimination or retaliation for making a claim. Following the logic of management culpability, Marshall (2005) studied the sexual harassment grievance process in a university setting. She found that management engaged in a variety of activities that discouraged the filing of sexual harassment claims. Frequently, supervisors would take the side of the harasser when a dispute arose, depicting the harassed as a troublemaker and placing organizational support behind the alleged offender. In doing so, supervisors often trivialized the conduct of the accused, and the accusers reported that supervisors might alter their job duties or even terminate their employment. Supervisors also discouraged reports by introducing nonexistent requirements into the sexual harassment policy, such as requiring the victim to confront her alleged accuser before filing a claim. Finally, Marshall found that supervisors interpreted the policy in a narrow and legalistic fashion that resulted in the dismissal of employee claims, diluting the protection ostensibly provided by the policy.

Women, in turn, learned of these employer practices, either through their own experiences or those of their colleagues (Marshall 2005). Knowledge of employers' reactions to complaints resulted in women discounting the grievance procedure as a method of securing their right to a harassment-free environment. The women, instead, usually confronted their harassers directly or decided to ignore their complaints. Women who did pursue remedies through the grievance process, typically only did so in particularly egregious cases and engaged in extensive litigation-like preparation for the lodging of the complaint (recording evidence, gathering witnesses, etc.).

Consequently, there are two primary results that arise as a consequence of these management-created obstacles. First, women are discouraged by institutional practices from filing sexual harassment claims. Second, and in tandem, the definition of what constitutes sexual harassment becomes very narrow because women are unlikely to make claims for actions that are not particularly egregious. In this way, management practices and women's responses to those practices, serve to both define women's access to rights, as well as to delineate the rights themselves. As raised in chapter 3, it appears that the absence of a clear legal definition of prohibited sexual harassment permits management and employees to develop their own definition of what constitutes discrimination.

This process of defining both rights and access to rights is described, and appears to occur, within the Greedy Associates community. Throughout this work, community members have described the dangers inherent in reporting sexual harassment or gender discrimination. Making such a report can be costly to one's career, as the attorney might be terminated or face difficulty in acquiring another position (see chapters 4 and 5). Further, little confidence is placed by community members in the ability of senior partners to remedy discrimination. Recommendations are made to women attorneys to gather extensive documentation and witnesses in case the need to report arises but, as highlighted in chapter 4, these women are nonetheless discouraged from lodging formal complaints; doing so, they are warned, could end one's career. Further, many attorneys described law firms as particularly hostile toward harassment or discrimination complaints, recounting a business culture that flagrantly disregards the very laws that its practitioners have sworn to uphold (chapter 5).

Thus, much as described by Marshall (2005) in her university study, the manner in which attorneys understand and pursue claims to rights is influenced by their particular institutional context. Sociologists have long understood that context matters in determining outcomes (see e.g., Durkheim [(1897) [1951]] on the influence of community type on anomie and suicide, and Entwisle, Alexander, and Olson [1994] on the influence of schools and neighborhoods on children's math scores). It is not simply one's individual characteristics that influence particular behaviors or outcomes; rather, the characteristics of the context in which that individual is nested are also determinative. Albiston (2005), like Marshall, observes that institutions play an important role in shaping both whether and how individuals will engage in rights mobilization. She emphasizes that institutional practices can serve to alter the very meaning of legal rights within the institution, perhaps narrowing or broadening the scope of the formal legal right. These practices, in the long run, become institutional norms that act to legitimate management actions. Thus, when management undertakes to create obstacles for employees in exercising their rights, employees' understandings of what their rights are and how they can be activated are constrained.

In addition to discouraging the filing of complaints, the organizational culture of the legal profession plays an important role in creating an environment that fosters gender discrimination. Members of the Greedy Associates community frequently describe law firms as a hostile, adversarial working environment, where coworkers are engaged in constant scheming and warring against one another to gain status and partner approval. One male attorney sets the scene for a large New York firm as follows:

> The partners gossip about and backstab each other so much that there is almost no way to figure out who's [sic] opinion has any weight. There are some givens, usually the self-involved egotistical male pigs who run departments. This place needs constant disparagement and backstabbing like a body needs water. Partners do it with each other, with clients and with associates.... A day isn't complete if professionalism isn't thrown out the window

in the spirit of ganging up to bring someone down. (*shearman suks*, 11246, 2/23/02)

Engaging in these activities improves an attorney's status, both through the actual act of disparagement, and through the comparison of the attorney engaging in the act with those he is criticizing (see additional discussion of disparagement in chapter 3). The type of environment revealed by these individuals suggests a predatory and abrasive occupation, dominated by male partners who encourage similar behavior by other male attorneys. At the heart of the problem for many female attorneys is, perhaps, an occupational culture that celebrates victories over those deemed as weak, and views women colleagues, like opposing counsel, as potential adversaries.

Consequently, occupational culture and management practices work in concert to both create an environment in which gender discrimination and harassment occurs and to suppress its opposition. In doing so, women attorneys are left with few options save to ignore the offensive behavior, or to leave their firm to try again elsewhere (see chapters 4 and 5). When women fail to challenge existing inequalities, however, the same consequences incur as found by Marshall (2005) in her university study—what is understood to be sexual harassment and gender discrimination remains narrow in scope because only the most egregious and well-documented situations are raised to management. This practice serves to reinforce management positions concerning the limited reach of gender discrimination laws. As a result, management's receptivity to gender discrimination claims, and associates' understandings of this receptivity, serve to shape both associates' pursuit of rights and, ultimately, institutional understandings of the rights themselves.

The Judicial System Discourages Rights Claims

Attorneys' rights consciousness is not simply influenced by their location within a particular occupational setting. Rather, their identity as professional legal actors renders important the viewpoints of the judicial system on gender discrimination and sexual harassment. These viewpoints are reflected in the legal decisions handed down by state and federal courts as well as in attorneys' interactions with judges in court. Although employees in other occupations might be familiar with judicial interpretation of state and federal law, their understanding of the law is likely to be founded more in lay beliefs than in case law. When it comes to some legal rights, an understanding of statutes and case law might serve to buttress an employee's rights claim. In the case of gender discrimination and harassment, however, intimate knowledge of judicial interpretation of the relevant laws serves to discourage claims.

The discussion in chapter 5 highlights the manner in which judicial interpretation of sexual harassment and gender discrimination laws appears to deviate substantially from the original intent of those laws. As MacKinnon (1979) emphasized, sexual harassment law will likely prove ineffective if it is written and interpreted absent an understanding of a woman's experience with harassment. The dominance of both male practitioners and a masculine legal professional culture (from which judges are drawn) appears to have garnered the exact result against which MacKinnon cautioned. Antidiscrimination laws continue to be interpreted in a manner that reflects a lack of awareness of the damage that can be inflicted by gender discrimination or harassment. This lack of understanding about the repercussions of discrimination and harassment results in decisions such as *Shepherd*, where the court determined that the work of a "reasonable person" would not be affected by repeated touchings and offensive comments (see discussion in chapter 5). Consequently, much of Title VII has been effectively undermined by the manner in which the courts have interpreted the law in sex discrimination and harassment cases.

The effects of these judicial decisions play out at both the management and associate level. Because law firm partners and associates are likely to be familiar with the judicial stance on gender discrimination and harassment, their understandings of the law and how it can be activated are altered. For law firm management, judicial decisions lend support to institutional practices of protecting a masculine organizational culture by discouraging discrimination and harassment claims. Indeed, attorneys in the Greedy Associates community described the manner in which law firm management was able to circumvent the effects of gender discrimination law by creating "performance based" reasons for termination or promotion decisions (chapter 5). An awareness of the loopholes created in the law by judicial decisions thereby enables management to both discourage claims and to more handily defeat claims when they arise.

Associates, on the other hand, are discouraged by judicial opinions that are frequently focused more on protecting the defendant rather than on the goals defined within gender discrimination and harassment law. The judicial system has created almost insurmountable obstacles for associates in establishing a claim of gender discrimination or harassment. Members of the Greedy Associates community describe the challenges posed by the law in establishing a claim, noting that it is virtually impossible to

establish a claim and that successful litigation is perhaps
dependent on whether the case involved assault (chapter 5).
As described in chapters 4 and 5, attorneys in the Web site
community are aware of these obstacles and, as a result,
are perhaps more likely to ignore discrimination than to
pursue a claim.

It appears that it is not simply management behavior
that discourages rights claims in the case of attorneys.
Rather, partners' and associates' intimate knowledge of
legal outcomes serves as a dampening effect on burgeon-
ing rights claims. Individuals in any occupation must
contend with the weakened protection wrought by judicial decision; consequently, formal litigation over gender
discrimination faces little chance of success for those in
all occupations. Judicial decisions, however, are likely to
play a much smaller role in *discouraging* claims for those
outside of the legal practice, where lay opinions about
the efficacy of the law dominate. Indeed, Nielsen (2003)
observes that media attention focused on litigation success creates a legal consciousness in the lay public that
plaintiffs achieve judicial victory in droves. This perception is not shared, however, by those within the legal profession, who know all too well the barriers to achieving
a win.

Female and Male Associates

Judicial decisions and management practices affect both
associates and management. What is perhaps not as readily
intuitive, however, is that judicial and management actions
regarding gender discrimination affect associates' employment situations, regardless of associate gender. Certainly
women face damaging repercussions from the "double

bind" of the legal profession, which simultaneously demands aggressive, predatory behavior, and labels women who engage in such behavior as unfeminine, butch, and lesbian (see e.g., Pierce 1995; chapters 3 and 5). Within the Greedy Associates community, though, it is not only women who describe the negative consequences of the masculine occupational culture, but men as well. As detailed in chapter 3, male attorneys describe an oppressive, hypermasculine environment that men are seemingly required to embrace or to suffer negative career repercussions. Male community members report facing management expectations that they will engage in sexual discussions concerning female associates, play sports or attend sporting events, and consume large quantities of alcohol (chapter 3).

Those who fail to do so face exclusion from networks and opportunities for advancement. As noted by one male attorney, "[g]ossiping, flirting and other garbage like that happens everywhere," but a male attorney was "labeled an outsider" if he "refus[ed] to take part in the unique...sports of gossiping, spreading rumors and disparaging others" (*shearman suks*, 11247, 2/23/02). Those who do participate in such activities, however, are perhaps rewarded, as highlighted by one community member's account of a lax attorney whose rehiring was attributed to his willingness to disparage female colleagues with the partners (chapter 3). Discourse in the Greedy Associates community, therefore, suggests that the same management actions that serve to foster a masculine culture and to discourage gender discrimination complaints, also place burdens on male associates. Like women, men are subject to the same power differentials existing between partner and associate and are similarly powerless to challenge contested practices.

Nonetheless, although men face the same pressures to conform to occupational norms, they are accepted if they choose to do so. As noted by Kilduff and Mehra (1996), men who achieve social dominance or power in a context that emphasizes male hegemony are likely to be admired as fulfilling expectations concerning male identity. They do not face the "double bind" experienced by women, who face negative repercussions regardless of whether they conform to occupational norms (Kilduff and Mehra 1996). Further, when men do engage in the expected behaviors, they do so at the expense of female associates. This results in yet another exercise of power, wherein male associates exert power over their female colleagues through disparagement and participation in masculine activities that send the message to female attorneys that they do not belong. These exercises of power appear to create an environment that fosters inequality and harassment and can also act to discourage the complaints of female associates. As described in chapter 4, some male attorneys in the Greedy Associates community suggest to female colleagues that sexual harassment policies are detrimental to the advancement of female associates, because the threat of harassment claims deters male partners from serving as their mentors. Further, only male attorneys in the Greedy Associates community suggested to sexual harassment victims that perhaps they were misinterpreting a harasser's actions (chapter 4). Viewpoints such as these create a further rift between male and female attorneys and can act to discourage complaints of harassment.

Women attorneys can also be deterred from pursuing a claim, however, by the reported experiences of other female associates. As found by Marshall (2005), when women learn of the negative experiences of other women in pursuing discrimination or harassment claims, they may opt not to proceed themselves. Indeed, in the Greedy Associates community, only identified women advised victims of sexual harassment to drop claims, often voicing their own negative experiences; one woman in the community vocalized her decision to do just that after hearing reports from other community members (see chapter 4). Thus, women attorneys can also discourage the claims of other women, and attorneys in the Greedy Associates community are no exception to this pattern.

The Greedy Associates Community: Dismantling Barriers to Rights Claims

The multilevel nature of the obstacles facing women's gender discrimination claims suggests that the maintenance of an unequal environment relies on the actions of many. Decisions made by judges act on both management and associates; management actions act directly on both male and female associates; and both male and female associates act on female associates. The analysis of legal discourse in the Greedy Associates community, however, suggests that the community has the potential to circumvent the multitiered forces that are acting in concert to discourage change in gender inequities.

The focus of this work has not been the identification of gender inequalities in the legal practice. Such investigations have been undertaken by many other researchers, using both representative and unrepresentative samples. Instead, this research has sought to examine the options available for challenging current gender inequalities in the legal practice and for forming new understandings and definitions of gender discrimination. In particular,

I have focused on whether and how interactions in an online community can play a role in activating the law to challenge unequal practices. This concluding chapter has reviewed various obstacles that, working together, serve to discourage changes in workplace practices, the filing of discrimination or harassment claims, and reformulations of definitions of discrimination. Given the recitation of these obstacles within the Internet community, community members are perhaps unlikely to turn to the formal complaint process or to pursue litigation; in other words, women face multiple barriers that dampen their ability to use tools ostensibly available for exercising their right to a discrimination-free workplace. Throughout this work, I have examined how workplace inequalities and harassment might be altered in the absence of these tools.

To equalize the experiences of male and female attorneys, it would seem that the occupational culture that promotes inequality must be altered by persuasion or by force. Frequently, encouraging voluntary change or compliance with the law fails, or results in the undermining of the original intent of the law itself (Ball, Krane, and Lauth 1982). As a result, more coercive tactics, such as litigation or the threat of other loss (pecuniary or loss of reputation), can prove more effective. To remedy gender discrimination in the legal practice, coercive tactics are perhaps those that will engender the most response from law firms. The most obvious coercive tactic—litigation—seems to have failed as a means for eliciting change in gender practices. This is due in part to obstacles discouraging the pursuit of litigation, as well as to the effect of unfriendly judicial interpretation of the law. The findings of this research, however, suggest that legal mobilization could still prove a useful tool in challenging gender inequality if it is used in the form of legal discourse.

Legal discourse appears to be a more promising resource for challenging and altering the legal practice than formal litigation. When used anonymously in the Greedy Associates community, legal discourse has the potential to prompt response, and perhaps change, from employers. Chapter 6 revealed that individuals in the community use legal discourse to challenge employers on gender issues and other working conditions. Further, they have used legal discourse in the community to contemplate the possibilities of collective organization, and to assert their right to use the community to voice complaints against their employers.

Legal discourse is an important means to challenge inequality, as it imbues claims with the authority of the law, lending an air of legitimacy to assertions of gender discrimination. Notably, community members label gender inequality as discriminatory even when the law has not clearly prohibited particular acts. This is significant on a number of levels. First, it emphasizes the fact that attorneys will often resort to legal discourse to assert claims to rights in a manner quite similar to laypersons. Despite their particular training in the law, attorneys will call upon general notions of equality to assert rights claims that do not exist on the books; this type of rights consciousness has been frequently discussed in terms of laypersons (see e.g., Marshall and Barclay 2003; Karst 1989), but not in the context of those trained in the law.

Second, the use of legal discourse to broadly label inequalities as discrimination is significant in that it takes a step toward redefining current conceptions of gender discrimination. This research has emphasized that the experiences and understandings of lawyers, in addition to laypersons, are at odds with current judicial and management interpretations of gender discrimination law. There is not simply a disconnect between judicial interpretation of the law and lay understandings of gender discrimination or harassment. Rather, those attorneys who have been trained in the field of law experience the same lack of connection between their everyday experiences with gender inequality and the remedies and rights afforded them by the formal litigation process. When attorneys use legal discourse to label "legal" practices as illegal gender discrimination, they emphasize the current disconnect between the law and workplace experience. More importantly, their categorization of these practices as illegal suggests a reformulation of gender discrimination. Legal discourse can be a particularly effective tool to achieve this end, as it allows attorneys to use a system embraced by their oppressors (other lawyers) as a vehicle for change.

Legal discourse on its own, however, would perhaps be ineffective, as it carries with it many of the same costs as litigation. The discourse becomes more valuable when used within the Greedy Associates community. This particular community, identified with the legal profession, provides a unique opportunity for the exercise of legal discourse. Community members are more apt to rely on legal discourse than individuals in other online communities, given their embeddedness in the legal profession. Further, their reliance on legal discourse perhaps has a greater air of legitimacy, as they are trained in the law and are viewed as experts and as legitimate lawmakers.

Through the Greedy Associates community, members are able to bypass many of the obstacles set in place by management and other associates, and find a voice to challenge inequalities. In particular, the anonymity the community provides its members enables them to challenge gender discrimination without endangering their employment or their status with their colleagues. Notably, it is not simply female associates who are empowered, but male associates as well. Men who are unable to challenge partners regarding oppressive, hypermasculine practices in the workplace are more apt to do so (and have done so) in an anonymous environment (see chapters 3–6).

In addition, the community allows attorneys to engage in a dialogue about gender inequality, both with one another and with those in positions of power. In other words, the community does not simply provide a forum for voicing complaints, but permits the response of others—those of an opposite gender, those whose experience with discrimination provides special insight, and those who are in management positions. In this way, the online environment permits a reversal of power relations, permitting attorneys to challenge management without fear of termination.

Community members are also able to rely on the knowledge and experience of other members—those who share knowledge regarding law firm culture, as well as knowledge regarding the efficacy and power of the law. Marshall (2005) observes that some employers train employees on how to encourage victims to raise issues concerning discrimination and harassment, and to arrive at possible solutions. She notes that "strategies such as these mobilize already existing gossip networks that disseminate valuable information" (Marshall 2005:119). In much the same way, interactions occurring in the Greedy Associates community could result in mobilization against gender inequality through the use of "existing gossip networks" that encourage the raising of issues of inequality, as well as the exploration of possible solutions. These solutions, as explored in chapters 4–6, have thus far ranged from litigation to the use of legal discourse to thoughts of unionization, as well as less overt strategies (one-on-one confrontation, using grievance procedures, etc.).

In addition to engaging in semiprotected, anonymous challenges to employer actions, the public nature of the Web site community further permits attorneys to use the threat of media exposure as an added weapon against their employers. Community members have noted the importance of the media in advancing the community's claims against employers. One male attorney described the media intervention in a particular dispute, stating that

> Tom Adcock from the N[ew] Y[ork] L[aw] J[ournal] did a good job but sounds like someone quickly shut him up. Maybe if the W[all] S[treet] J[ournal] or the N[ew] Y[ork] T[imes] wants a crack they should try and see if these whiners are real. If you have some idea how we could move this discussion off of this board and give it to some authority to investigate the firm's employment, sexual harassment and general ethical practices, then speak up and the rest of us will wait for the results of the investigation. (S&S Survivor, 8168, 11/08/01)

At a later date, the same male attorney encouraged the media to investigate the practices at a law firm, stating that

> Bottom line, let the N[ew] Y[ork] L[aw] J[ournal] or W[all] S[treet] J[ournal] take a free walk around, form their own opinion, and call it a day. (9187, 12/03/01)

Another community member observed that "nothing's better than some publicity about a large firm that hates women" (Gammon1, 29665, 1/24/07). Using the community to invite media investigation does appear to be viewed as an additional source of power for attorneys in the community.

And, as noted in chapter 4, the media do visit the Greedy Associates Web site to obtain the "inside scoop" about law firm activities. Some reporters visit the Web site to actively solicit responses on particular issues. For instance, one New York reporter stated, "I'm a legal reporter at *Bloomberg News*, trolling the message board for stories. Here's my contact info if you've got one" (*oldskoolgreedy*, 14561, 8/28/02). Another reporter echoed the invitation, soliciting community members to "Call me any time. Confidentiality guaranteed" (*thomas adcock*, 14620, 9/04/2002). In response to an article published about a firm that drew on comments in the community, one community member stated, "I want to thank [the author] for giving a voice to those who had not had one. I know firsthand that there have been problems at this firm for a long time....I take solace in the fact that these slimy partners are finally getting the bad press they deserve" (*friendofassoc.*, 7766, 11/01/01).

Community members not only welcome the media for the potential to open a more public dialogue on controversies, but also take note of the power of the media to place pressure on offending law firms. As one attorney aptly summarized, it is "[i]nteresting that those disguised [firm] partners jump up to attack us when we have something to say, but run for cover when it's a reporter" (*S&S Survivor*, 9801, 12/14/01). This individual goes on to essentially implore the media to pressure law firms to respond more publicly to associate complaints stating that "[w]e never said everything that we hear was confirmed three times over. That is why we asked [the firm], over and over again, to invite a third party in to look at the facts.

How far to push that point is now also mostly in the hands of journalists" (9801, 12/14/01).

Perhaps, therefore, the efficacy of the Greedy Associates Web site in eliciting change for women attorneys is dependent in part on the public pressuring firms for responses to associates' claims of rights violations. Claims of sexual harassment and other law violations have a significant potential to damage a law firm's reputation. By using legal discourse to lend an air of legitimacy to claims, members of the community can both prompt employer response, and perhaps encourage an alteration in gender practices in law firms. If statements within the community itself do not serve as a powerful enough force, the media will perhaps amplify the voices of community members, serving to bring the issue of gender discrimination into the court of public opinion.

The Future of the Community

Future interactions within the Greedy Associates community, as well as external responses to those interactions, will reveal the full potential of community discourse for challenging gender discrimination. Findings from this research demonstrate that gender issues are raised in the community, that advice is offered, that interactions have the potential to affect an attorney's handling of inequalities, and that management takes note of and participates in these exchanges. Further, attorneys use legal discourse in the community to challenge both working conditions and gender issues. Whether the use of this discourse will have any effect on gender-related practices, however, remains to be seen.

Effects of community discourse could be subtle, as participants' attitudes concerning gender-related issues might be gradually altered due to exposure to community discourse. On the other hand, in situations where community discourse has been inflammatory and of a long duration, the effects might be much more dramatic. It is possible that employers have altered management practices in direct response to discourse occurring in the Greedy Associates community, or as a result of subsequent media and public pressure. Examining how community discourse plays out *outside of* the community, therefore, could provide important insight into the extent of its power in effecting change.

Further, the community may also play a future role in exposing and addressing the experiences of male attorneys. Although it is women who predominantly experience discrimination and harassment (Nielsen 2000; Rosenberg, Perlstadt, and Phillips 1993), not all male attorneys are content with their assigned gender roles within the legal practice. Many male attorneys in the Greedy Associates community described situations in which they seemed to find themselves forced to comply with the gender expectations of management (chapters 3–6). Their stories reveal that other male identities are subordinated to that of hegemonic masculinity and are, as a result, unlikely to be expressed in the legal profession (Connell 1995). Male associates, much like female associates, are thus faced with a sense of powerlessness connected with defining their gender identities; this powerlessness can perhaps be subverted by participation in the Greedy Associates community.

In addition, the community appears to serve as a vehicle to expose gender inequalities to both male and female attorneys; attorneys of both sexes are then afforded an opportunity to unite (via legal discourse or other means) against such inequalities. Research focused on women's labor movements has found that women's success in seeking benefits increases when they emphasize that both women's and men's interests coincide and that, when men protect women's rights, they are protecting the rights of all of the working class (Milkman 1987). Consequently, if female associates are able to draw upon the dissatisfaction of male associates with the current organizational culture of the legal practice, then a greater potential for change could result. Within the Greedy Associates community, there is already evidence of male and female associates banding together to oppose partners in terms of working conditions, the right to participate in the Web site community, and unionization (see chapter 6). Thus, associates can and have united to work toward issues that impact the "greater good" of their profession; the key will be in focusing these joint activities on issues more directly bearing on occupational culture and gender.

Finally, a continued observation of the Greedy Associates community will reveal, in the coming years, if the community members take further advantage of the potential of the Web site for challenging employer practices generally, and gender discrimination particularly. The community has already transitioned from one focused on salary issues to one in which the presence of "off-topic" conversations dominates the board; this transition demonstrates the ability of the community to develop to meet emerging needs. These factors lend promise to the notion that the board could evolve once more, into a community more consciously focused on legal mobilization and the use of legal discourse.

Notably, using legal discourse in the community addresses one of the major critiques of Critical Legal Scholars (CLS) regarding the ability of legal mobilization to effect change. CLS argue that legal mobilization is problematic because it is focused on individual harms and individual remedies (Crenshaw 1995; Scheingold 1974). When legal discourse is used in the Web site community, however, mobilization for change in gender practices extends beyond the individual. Mobilization occurs on behalf of both male and female associates, and those working in firms throughout the country (and indeed, throughout the world). Further, there is the potential to affect understandings of gender issues in the legal practice for judges, partners, associates, and laypersons. The possible reach of this mobilization tool is limitless, imbuing employee conversations at the "information age watercooler" with an unexpected and profound power. The coming years will reveal whether this power comes to its full fruition in the Greedy Associates community.

Notes

2 Methods—Exploring an Internet Community

1. Although online communities offer some means of deconstructing these boundaries, many argue that individuals bring offline identities and understandings with them when they enter online communities (Kendall 2002; Kendall 2000; Warhol 1999). As a result, the concept of the Internet as a utopian society, where gender, race, class, and geography are irrelevant, overstates the ability to escape offline identities.
2. The Web site name has a 2000 copyright, although the first post is dated August 1999.
3. Messages from the Internet community will be cited with the members' online handle, followed by the message number, and the date.
4. For details regarding calculation of this estimate, please see appendix 2.1.
5. It is undoubtedly true, for instance, that a number of the messages analyzed within this text were drafted by members of the Shearman & Sterling law firm. There was a notable timeframe in which attorneys from this firm dominated the community, as the firm was experiencing a variety of public economic and social crises. The prevalence of Shearman attorneys certainly make some of the statements unrepresentative of attorneys as a whole. Nonetheless, this becomes less relevant given that the analysis is focused on the discourse occurring in the community and the possible effects of the community on the progression of the dispute process.
6. Even if the individual does self-identify, there is always room for doubt, since the Internet allows for a disembodiment that can result in individuals engaging in gender switching (O'Farrell and Vallone 1999; Kendall 2002). Researchers studying members of Web site communities both online and offline have found, however, that gender switching does not occur often and, when it does, the members often reveal their true identity over the course of time (Kendall 2002).
7. For more detailed discussion of gendered conversational styles in online communities, see section titled "A Theory of Cybercommunication."
8. Notably, recent research has consistently found no gender gap concerning access to the Internet, although there are gender differences in how frequently the Internet is used or for what purposes (Wasserman and Richmond-Abbott 2005; Ono and Zavodny 2003; Bimber 2000).

9. It is important to note, however, that some of the behaviors that are labeled as displays of "feminine" or "masculine" conversational styles on the Internet occur in forums that are dominated by either gender. Gatson and Zweerink (Under Review), for instance, observe that when individuals demonstrate a concern with online etiquette, such behavior is typically seen as feminine. They point out, however, that voicing a concern regarding the proper manner in which to interact in a Web site community is simply a common part of Internet culture, engaged in by both males and females. They cite, for example, one instance in a fan-based community in which it was two males in the community who censured the inappropriate behavior of another individual. In this manner, although certain online behaviors have been characterized as "feminine" or "masculine," some of these behaviors can transcend the gender line.

10. As discussed in chapter 3, community members' experiences with gender discrimination do seem to parallel the experiences reported by attorneys selected through representative samples for interviews or surveys.

3   Gender Inequality in the Legal Practice

1. Past researchers have assessed discrimination faced by women attorneys primarily by conducting surveys or interviews.

2. Indeed, research comparing data obtained through Internet surveys to data gleaned through offline surveys found few significant differences in either the sample composition or the survey responses, despite the varying methods of administering the survey (Ross et al., 2005).

3. One might notice that numerous excerpts are taken throughout this chapter from the post by *shearman suks* made on February 23, 2002. Within this one message, *shearman suks* discusses virtually all of the elements of gender inequality within the legal practice, particularly those that pertain to the gossip network. Consequently, I have repeatedly made use of portions of his message within this chapter, combining his rather expansive comments with those made by other members of the community.

5   Employing Litigation to Redress Gender Inequality

1. Summary judgment entails a process by which a party files a motion requesting the judge to enter judgment in their favor as a matter of law, as there are no genuine issues of material fact that are in dispute. If judgment is rendered at this stage, the case concludes without a trial.

2. Clearly, searches conducted in legal databases are apt to miss cases that could be on point, but which do not contain the requested search terms. As such, I do not claim that the search results I report here encompass all decisions rendered on this matter; this is merely a fairly complete sample of employment discrimination decisions involving women attorneys.

6   Lawyers Using Legal Discourse to Challenge Gender Discrimination

1. Although the First Amendment offers no protection in this case, labor law—as discussed previously—might provide some protection of collective employee action.

References

Acker, Joan. 1990. "Hierarchies, Jobs, Bodies: A Theory of Gendered Organizations." *Gender and Society* 4:139–158.

Albiston, Catherine. 2005. "Bargaining in the Shadow of Social Institutions: Competing Discourses and Social Change in Workplace Mobilization of Civil Rights." *Law and Society Review* 39:11–49.

Altman, Andrew. 1990. *Critical Legal Studies: A Liberal Critique.* Princeton, NJ: Princeton University Press.

Ames, Genevieve M., and Linda-Anne Rebhun. 1993. "Woman, Alcohol and Work: Interactions of Gender, Ethnicity and Occupational Culture." *Social Science and Medicine* 43:1649–1663.

Baer, Judith. 1999. *Our Lives before the Law.* Princeton, NJ: Princeton University Press.

Ball, Howard, Dale Krane, and Thomas P. Lauth. 1982. *Compromised Compliance: Implementation of the 1965 Voting Rights Act.* Westport, CT: Greenwood Press.

Baumle, Amanda K., and Mark Fossett. 2005. "Statistical Discrimination in Employment: Its Practice, Conceptualization, and Implications for Public Policy." *American Behavioral Scientist* 48:1250–1274.

Baym, Nancy K. 1995. "The Emergence of Community in CMC." In *CyberSociety: Computer-Mediated Communication and Community,* edited by Steven G. Jones, 138–163. Thousand Oaks, CA: Sage.

———. 2000. *Tune in, Log on: Soaps, Fandom, and Online Community.* Thousand Oaks, CA: Sage.

Betz, Michael, and Lenahan O'Connell. 1989. "Work Orientations of Males and Females: Exploring the Gender Socialization Approach." *Sociological Inquiry* 59:318–330.

Biddle, Jeff E., and Daniel Hamermesh. 1998. "Beauty, Productivity and Discrimination: Lawyers' Looks and Lucre." *Journal of Labor Economics* 16:172–201.

Bimber, Bruce. 2000. "Measuring the Gender Gap on the Internet." *Social Science Quarterly* 81:868–876.

Bourdieu, Pierre, and John Thompson. 1991. *Language and Symbolic Power.* Cambridge, MA: Harvard University Press.

Civil Rights Act of 1964, Title VII, 42 U.S.C. § 2000e.

Connell, R. W. 1987. *Gender and Power: Society, the Person, and Sexual Politics*. Sydney: Allen and Unwin.

———. 1995. *Masculinities*. Berkeley: University of California Press.

Crenshaw, Kimberle. 1995. "Race, Reform, and Retrenchment: Transformation and Legitimation in Antidiscrimination Law." In *Critical Legal Thought: An American-German Debate*, edited by Christian Joerges and David M. Trubek, 103–122. Baden-Baden, Germany: Nomos.

Durkheim, Émile. [1897] 1951. *Suicide: A Study in Sociology*. Glencoe, IL: Free Press of Glencoe.

Emmett, Robert. 1982. "VNET or GRIPENET." *Datamation* 4:48–58.

Entwisle, Doris R., Karl L. Alexander, and Linda S. Olson. 1994. "The Gender Gap in Math: Its Possible Origins in Neighborhood Effects." *American Sociological Review* 59:822–838.

Epstein, Cynthia F. 1970. "Encountering the Male Establishment: Sex-Status Limits on Women's Careers in the Professions." *American Journal of Sociology* 75:6.

Ewick, Patricia, and Susan Silbey. 1998. *The Common Place of Law: Stories from Everyday Life*. Chicago, IL: University of Chicago Press.

Feagin, Joe, and Douglas Eckberg. 1980. "Discrimination: Motivation, Action, Effects, and Context." *Annual Review of Sociology* 6:1–20.

Felstiner, William, Richard Abel, and Austin Sarat. 1980–1981. "The Emergence and Transformation of Disputes: Naming, Blaming, Claiming...." *Law and Society Review* 15:631–654.

Fernback, Jan. 1999. "There Is a There There: Notes toward a Definition of Cybercommunity." In *Doing Internet Research: Critical Issues and Methods for Examining the Net*, edited by Steven G. Jones, 203–220. Thousand Oaks, CA: Sage.

Finholt, Thomas, and Lee Sproull. 1990. "Electronic Groups at Work." *Organizational Science* 1:4164.

Fitzgerald v. Ford, Marrin, Esposito, Witmeyer and Gleser, 153 F.Supp.2d. 219 (D.C. S.D.N.Y. 2001).

Fitzgerald, Louise, and Suzanne Swan. 1995. "Why Didn't She Just Report Him?: The Psychological and Legal Inclinations of Women's Responses to Sexual Harassment." *Journal of Social Issues* 51:117–138.

Gatson, Sarah N., and Amanda Zweerink. 2000. "Choosing Community: Rejecting Anonymity in Cyberspace." *Research in Community Sociology* 10:105–137.

———. 2004a. *Interpersonal Culture on the Internet: Television, the Internet, and the Making of a Community*. Lewiston, NY: Edwin Mellen Press.

———. 2004b. "'Natives' Practicing and Inscribing Community: Ethnography Online." *Qualitative Research* 4:179–200.

———. Under Review. "Gender Practices in an Internet Community: Reproduction or Re-Vamping?"

Gerson, Kathleen. 1985. *Hard Choices: How Women Decide about Work, Career, and Motherhood*. Berkeley: University of California Press.

Gifford, Rob. 2005. "Internet Tests Chinese Political Controls." Retrieved on February 28, 2005 (http://www.npr.org/templates/story/story.php?storyId=4504864).

Goldin, Claudia. 1990. *Understanding the Gender Gap*. New York: Oxford University Press.

Hall v. Gus Coast Co., 842 F.2d 1010 (8th Cir. 1988).

Hearn, Jeff, and P. Wendy Parkin. 1987. *Sex at Work: The Power and the Paradox of Organization Sexuality*. New York: St. Martin.

Hull, Kathleen E., and Robert L. Nelson. 2000. "Assimilation, Choice, or Constraint? Testing Theories of Gender Differences in the Careers of Lawyers." *Social Forces* 79:1.

Jefferson, Gail. 1988. "On the Sequential Organization of Troubles-talk in Ordinary Conversation." *Social Problems* 35:418–441.

Jones, Steve G. 1999. "Studying the Net: Intricacies and Issues." In *Doing Internet Research: Critical Issues and Methods for Examining the Net*, edited by Steven G. Jones, 1–27. Thousand Oaks, CA: Sage.

Kanter, Rosabeth Moss. 1977. *Men and Women of the Corporation*. New York: Basic Books.

Karst, Kenneth. 1989. *Belonging to America: Equal Citizenship and the Constitution*. New Haven, CT: Yale University Press.

Kendall, Lori. 1999. "Recontextualizing 'Cyberspace': Methodological Considerations for Online Research." In *Doing Internet Research: Critical Issues and Methods for Examining the Net*, edited by Steven G. Jones, 57–74. Thousand Oaks, CA: Sage.

———. 2000. "'Oh No! I'm a NERD!' Hegemonic Masculinity on an Online Forum." *Gender and Society* 14:256–274.

———. 2002. *Hanging out in the Virtual Pub: Masculinities and Relationships Online*. Berkeley: University of California Press.

Kilduff, Martin, and Ajay Mehra. 1996. "Hegemonic Masculinity among the Elite: Power, Identity, and Homophily in Social Networks." In *Masculinities in Organizations*, edited by Cliff Cheng, 115–129. Thousand Oaks, CA: Sage.

Leahy, Terry. 1994. "Taking up a Position: Discourses of Femininity and Adolescence in the Context of Man/Girl Relationships." *Gender and Society* 8:48–72.

Lee, Orville. 2001. "Legal Weapons for the Weak? Democratizing the Force of Words in an Uncivil Society." *Law and Social Inquiry* 26:847–892.

Levin, Jack, and William Levin. 1982. *The Functions of Discrimination and Prejudice* (2nd ed.). New York: Harper and Row.

MacKinnon, Catherine A. 1979. *Sexual Harassment of Working Women: A Case of Sex Discrimination*. New Haven, CT: Yale University Press.

Marini, Margaret M., and Mary Brinton. 1984. "Sex Typing in Occupational Socialization." In *Sex Segregation in the Workplace: Trends, Explanations, Remedies*, edited by Barbara F. Reskin, 192–232. Washington, DC: National Academy Press.

Marini, Margaret M., Pi-ling Fan, and Erica Finley. 1996. "Gender and Job Values." *Sociology of Education* 69:49–65.

Marshall, Anna-Maria. 2005. "Idle Rights: Employees' Rights Consciousness and the Construction of Sexual Harassment Policies." *Law and Society Review* 39:83–123.

Marshall, Anna-Maria, and Scott Barclay. 2003. "In their Own Words: How Ordinary People Construct the Legal World." *Law and Social Inquiry* 28:617–628.

Mather, Lynn, and Barbara Yngvesson. 1981. "Language, Audience, and the Transformation of Disputes." *Law and Society Review* 15:775–821.

McCann, Michael. 1994. *Rights at Work: Pay Equity Reform and the Politics of Legal Mobilization*. Chicago, IL: University of Chicago Press.

McEvoy, Arthur F. 2005. "A New Realism for Legal Studies." *Wisconsin Law Review* 2:443–454.

Mertz, Elizabeth. 1992. "Language, Law, and Social Meanings: Linguistic/ Anthropological Contributions to the Study of Law." *Law and Society Review* 26:413–445.

Milkman, Ruth. 1987. *Gender at Work: The Dynamics of Job Segregation by Sex during World War II*. Chicago: University of Illinois Press.

Miller, Laura L. 1997. "Not Just Weapons of the Weak: Gender Harassment as a Form of Protest for Army Men." *Social Psychology Quarterly* 60:32–51.

Miller, Richard E., and Austin Sarat. 1980–1981. "Grievances, Claims, and Disputes: Assessing the Adversary Culture." *Law and Society Review* 15:525–566.

Mizrach, Steve. n.d. "What Is Cyberanthropology?" Retrieved on April 20, 2003 (http://www.fiu.edu/~mizrachs/Cyber Anthropology.html).

Nelson, Robert L., and William P. Bridges. 1999. *Legalizing Gender Inequality: Courts, Markets, and Unequal Pay for Women in America*. New York: Cambridge University Press.

Nielsen, Laura Beth. 2000. "Situating Legal Consciousness: Experiences and Attitudes of Ordinary Citizens about Law and Street Harassment." *Law and Society Review* 34:1055–1090.

———. 2003. *Media Misrepresentation?: Antidiscrimination Law, Print Media, and Legal Consciousness*. Chicago, IL: American Bar Foundation.

O'Farrell, M. A., and L. Vallone, eds. 1999. *Virtual Gender: Fantasies of Subjectivity and Embodiment*. Ann Arbor: University of Michigan Press.

Omi, Michael, and Howard Winant. 1994. *Racial Formation in the United States: From the 1960s to the 1980s*. New York: Routledge.

Ono, Hiroshi, and Madeline Zavodny. 2003. "Gender and the Internet." *Social Science Quarterly* 84:111–121.

Pierce, Jennifer L. 1995. *Gender Trials: Emotional Lives in Contemporary Law Firms*. Los Angeles: University of California Press.

Pliskin, Nava, and Celia Romm. 1994. "Empowerment Effects of Electronic Group Communication: A Case Study." Work. Pap. Dep. Manage., Faculty Commerce, University of Wollongong, Australia.

Pomerantz, Anita. 1978. "Attributions of Responsibility: Blamings." *Sociology* 12:115–121.

Price Waterhouse v. Hopkins, 490 U.S. 228 (1989).

Quinn, Beth A. 2000. "The Paradox of Complaining: Law, Humor, and Harassment in the Everyday Work World." *Law and Social Inquiry* 25:1151–1185.

Reskin, Barbara, and Irene Padavic. 1994. *Women and Men at Work*. Thousand Oaks, CA: Pine Forge Press.

Rheingold, Howard. 1993. *The Virtual Community: Homesteading on the Electronic Frontier*. Reading, MA: Addison-Wesley.

Rhode, Deborah L. 2001. *The Unfinished Agenda: Women in the Legal Profession*. Chicago, IL: American Bar Association Commission on Women in the Profession.

Rosenberg, Janet, Harry Perlstadt, and William R. F. Phillips. 1993. "Now That We Are Here: Discrimination, Disparagement, and Harassment at Work and the Experience of Women Lawyers." *Gender and Society* 7:415–433.

Ross, Michael W., Sven-Axel Mansson, Kristian Daneback, Al Cooper, and Ronny Tikkanen. 2005. "Biases in Internet Sexual Health Samples: Comparison of an Internet Sexuality Survey and a National Sexual Health Survey in Sweden." *Social Science and Medicine* 61:245–252.

Sarat, Austin D., and William L. F. Felstiner. 1988. "Law and Social Relations: Vocabularies of Motive in Lawyer/Client Interaction." *Law and Society Review* 22:737–770.

Scheingold, Stuart A. 1974. *The Politics of Rights: Lawyers, Public Policy, and Political Change*. New Haven, CT: Yale University Press.

Schneider, Elizabeth M. 1990. "The Dialectic of Rights and Policies: Perspectives from the Women's Movement." In *Women, the State, and Welfare*, edited by Linda Gordon, 235–248. Madison: Wisconsin University Press.

Sharf, Barbara. 1997. "Communicating Breast Cancer On-Line: Support and Empowerment on the Internet." *Women and Health* 26:65–84.

———. 1999. "Beyond Netiquette: The Ethics of Doing Naturalistic Discourse Research on the Internet." In *Doing Internet Research: Critical Issues and Methods for Examining the Net*, edited by Steven G. Jones, 243–256. Thousand Oaks, CA: Sage.

Shepherd v. The Comptroller of Public Accounts of the State of Texas, 168 F.3d. 871 (5th Cir. 1999).

Shore, Elsie R. 2001. "Relationships between Drinking and Type of Practice among U.S. Female and Male Attorneys." *Journal of Social Psychology* 141:650–659.

Silberman, Steve. 1998. "First Amendment? Not on the Job." *Wired News*. Retrieved on November 11, 2003 (http://www.wired.com/news/politics/0,1283,10217,00.html).

Sokoloff, Natalie J. 1992. *Black Women and White Women in the Professions: Occupational Segregation by Race and Gender, 1960–1980*. New York: Routledge.

Trice, Harrison M., and Paul M. Roman. 1978. *Spirits and Demons at Work: Alcohol and Other Drugs on the Job.* Ithaca, NY: Cornell University Press.

Trice, Harrison M., and William J. Sonnenstuhl. 1990. "On the Construction of Drinking Norms in Work Organizations." *Journal of Studies on Alcohol* 51:201–220.

Tushnet, Mark. 1984. "An Essay on Rights." *Texas Law Review* 62:1363–1364.

Unger, Roberto. 1989. *The Critical Legal Studies Movement.* Boston, MA: Harvard University Press.

U.S. Merit Systems and Protection Board. 1988. *Sexual Harassment in the Federal Government: An Update.* Washington, DC.

Warf, Barney, and John Grimes. 1997. "Counterhegemonic Discourses and the Internet." *Geographical Review* 87:259–274.

Warhol, Robyn. 1999. "The Inevitable Virtuality of Gender: Performing Femininity on an Electronic Bulletin Board for Soap Opera Fans." In *Virtual Gender: Fantasies of Subjectivity and Embodiment*, edited by M. A. O'Farrell and L. Vallone, 91–107. Ann Arbor: University of Michigan Press.

Wasserman, Ira M., and Marie Richmond-Abbott. 2005. "Gender and the Internet: Causes of Variation in Access, Level, and Scope of Use." *Social Science Quarterly* 86:252–270.

Wellman, Barry, Janet Salaff, Dimitrina Dimitrova, Laura Garton, Milena Gulia, and Caroline Haythornwaite. 1996. "Computer Networks as Social Networks: Collaborative Work, Telework, and Virtual Community." *Annual Review of Sociology* 22:213–238.

Yngvesson, Barbara. 1993. "Beastly Neighbors: Continuing Relations in Cattle Country." *Yale Law Journal* 102:1787–1801.

Zuboff, Shoshana. 1988. *In the Age of the Smart Machine.* New York: Basic Books.

Index